DRIVEN TO SUCCEED

The Life and Philosophy
of Entrepreneur, Q.L. Snook, Sr.

Copyright 1997 by Quentin Laurence Snook, Sr.

ISBN #: 1-884707-56-4
Library of Congress Cataloging-in-Publication
data pending

Driven to Succeed, as told to Steven L. Mundahl, is:

Printed in the USA by
Lifestyles Press
P.O. Box 1140
Tavares, FL 32778
(352) 742-2155

Dedication

This book is dedicated to the loving memory of my parents, Genevieve and Clayton M. Snook, Sr., my wife's parents, Iva and Earl McArthy and to my wife, Margaret, and our children: Larry, Maurice, Tom, Sarah and Earl, and their families.

Preface

My primary motivation for publishing this book comes from a strong desire to help those who have decided to start their own business to succeed.

I have witnessed in my lifetime, from the days of the Great Depression, many businesses succeed and many fail. Over ninety percent of all business activity in the United States comes from small businesses with fewer than 100 employees. Statistics reveal that for every ten new businesses, eight will fail within five years.

While I was with Service Corp of Retired Executives (SCORE) for ten years, I worked with approximately 100 clients. In many cases, the qualifications necessary for success were lacking.

I have the hope that this book will help to reduce the high failure rate of new businesses. This book will encourage eager and willing entrepreneurs to form a business using minimal capital, maintaining control with non-convertible "B" stock, and have a ready-made market for their product or service. I hope too, that the book will show what an important role a few private investors can play in assisting in quickly starting the new company.

Thanks go to my parents, Hartwell Howard, Rodger Bliss, who is my respected friend with his own unique success story, the three Mackle brothers, who developed many cities in Florida including where we live in Deltona, and Neil Bahr, cofounder of the Deltona Corporation, with his great ability to help others succeed.

Furthermore, I'd like to recognize Jeb Bush for his ability and success in coauthoring *Profiles in Character*. Everyone will be motivated upon reading Jeb's views on character. I have also been inspired by Dr. Oscar Plumb's book, *A Search for Christian Identity*, Dr. Robert Schuller,

If It's Going To Be, It's Up To Me, a guide to salvation and living. These books are must reading.

Thanks many times over to the publishers of my book, Steve Mundahl and his wife, Sandy, and their daughter Krista, as well as their staff of dedicated people at Lifestyles Press, whose desire is to serve their clients well.

I want to acknowledge the serendipitous occurrences I have had from my forty-eight year membership in the Kiwanis Club of Champaign-Urbana, Illinois. I could write another book on just my Noon Club experiences with Kiwanis.

The inspiration to write this book is to share my experiences to help others succeed. The profit motive did not surface during the writing of this book; in fact, all proceeds will go to charity, with special consideration to the Noon Champaign-Urbana, Illinois Kiwanis Club, to which I owe much in nonmaterial compensation.

Thank you to each friend, associate and family member for sharing their comments.

It has been written, "To him that much has been given, much is required."

I would amend that to say, "Much more is required!"

Q.L.S.

Table of Contents

1   Building Drive for Success 1
    All basic wealth comes from labor 3
    We do it all for our family 14
    I just knew that I never wanted to be poor 19
    Waste not, want not 24
    The driving energy of most people is fear of loss 30
    I never wanted to work for someone else 35
    Comments 41

2   Gathering Tools for Success 43
    Learn to listen and listen to learn 45
    The role of providence 50
    Be determined 55
    A motive for profit 74
    Comments 75

3   Forming Successful Relationships 77
    Margaret Snook and the importance of a good marriage 79
    Satisfied clients can open doors to prospects 83
    Relationships in the military 94
    Maintain an honest relationship with the Creator 98
    Comments 108

4   Making a Commitment to Succeed 111
    New heights in life insurance 113
    The Q.L. Snook Securities Company 119
    General Development Corp. & the Mackle Bros. 123
    Manage your future 138
    When it no longer fits, it's time to walk away 166
    Comments 180

5   The Joy of Giving 183
    A time to reflect 185
    A Legion of Honor 188
    The gift of family 200
    Comments 204

6   The Business Philosophy of Q.L. Snook 207
    Seven key elements to entrepreneurial success 209
    Building blocks for success 228
    Comments 232
    Personal and professional milestones 248

Photo Album 251

1

BUILDING DRIVE FOR SUCCESS

All basic wealth comes from labor

Quentin Laurence Snook was born on December 11, 1922 in Normal, Illinois. He was one of seven children, having three brothers and three sisters. Snook's mother, Genevieve, and father, Clayton, were pioneers who had settled in America to farm their land.

His childhood home was a large two-story house on acreage large enough to have a big family garden, a chicken coop and a couple of outbuildings where his father stored equipment.

Quentin's father, Clayton Snook, had been a farmer. The family had lost three farms due mainly to the economics of the time. Like so many others, Clayton took what jobs were available to feed and house his family.

"I remember many dinners that we ate boiled dandelion greens and popcorn," says Snook. "Even popcorn was a treat usually reserved for Sundays. We didn't have any money, but then no one did. Well, no one that lived near us, that is."

Although poor, the Snooks were not as poor as many during the early years of the Great Depression in America. His father always seemed to find a job and kept his family fed. There wasn't extra money for many things, however, and whatever young Quentin wanted as a child, he had to earn. This idea of having to earn everything he wanted, would become a philosophy that would stay with him for the rest of his life.

"As a kid, I saw other children in the area on bicycles, and I surely wanted one. I dreamed of it, and was obsessed by it. So, I asked my dad to buy me one." His father's response didn't really surprise him much. "He listened and nodded his head up and down as I told him how badly I wanted and needed one. I really was pretty good as I gave my reasons!"

Snook's father agreed that Quentin should have a bike. Then he received one of many loving lessons he learned from his dad. Times were hard. There was no extra money to purchase a bicycle. But even if there were, would Quentin want to take the few dollars saved by his father in case of dire emergency to spend on a bicycle? The few dollars saved by his mother and father could be the sliver of a difference between the hobos that rode the rails through rural Illinois in search of a meal, and survival for the family. Jobs were scarce, his father told him. There was no guarantee that he could hold on to his job. He could be laid off like so many others. Would it be fair to his mother and brothers and sisters that the family's meager savings be spent on a bicycle for Quentin?

There was no need for further discussion. Young Snook saw the wisdom in that argument. Although that bicycle had been the most important thing to him in his young life, nothing was more important than the welfare of the family. Nothing was more vital than the ability of his father to put food on the table and keep a roof over his children's heads. No, if he wanted that bicycle, he couldn't expect anyone to *just give it to him!* He'd just have to find another way.

His father's explanation was a loving and careful one. That's the way he remembers his mother and father: caring and sensitive to his feelings. The welfare of our family was first, not the welfare of any one individual. No self-indulgence was worth the risk of breaking that often thin thread that bound the American family in the Depression. It was the reason for his parents to tell him that alcohol, smoking, laziness and any other indulgence couldn't be tolerated. It would tear at the glue that held the family together. It made sense to him. The argument really didn't have to be preached to him often. He understood that every time he and his brothers and sisters sat down over a meal that the food before him had come from sacrifice and hard work. He also understood that everyone in that house did their part to keep the family together and working. It was the way he grew up.

Growing up, Snook can remember that the house lamps were lit with gas from a source buried in the yard. It was a major event when the local power company put up poles along Route 51 and right beside their home. When electricity came, the Snooks added a new refrigerator and stove and, of course, electric lights.

"In our attic we had a water tank to fill wash bowls in each bedroom, our kitchen and our 1-1/2 baths, as well as the basement tub. Our deep well had its own pump house for controls. We also had a coal-

5

stoked furnace with ducts to heat all fourteen rooms in our house."

Snook's parents purchased the house in the 1920s and it remained in their family until his mother sold the homestead in 1961.

"We all had chores," Q.L. remembered. "One of mine was to empty the ashes from the stove every night and refill the buckets with corn cobs and coal so mother would be able to heat water and cook breakfast. I did it every night. Even when I wanted to do so many other things, I wasn't about to disappoint my mother and not have those buckets filled when she got up. No, sir. I wanted to do my part. It was important."

Besides stove duties, Quentin fed the chickens and cleaned rabbit hutches every day after school. Chores, homework and school filled his day. There wasn't a lot of time to try to earn money for that bicycle, but he knew he'd find a way.

Quentin also took whatever odd jobs were available to him, fitting them in between school, chores and other jobs. He became obsessive about managing his time, and undertook every job with vigor and enthusiasm.

He remembers reading in the paper an advertisement for salespeople to sell *the miracle salve. Perfect for any ailment!* The company advertising it was called the Attica Salve Company.

"I asked my dad about it and pointed out where the ad said: *Earn big commissions!* Boy, that spoke to me! But, my dad didn't say much. It was just like him; he didn't encourage or discourage me. He just sort of left it up to me."

Quentin had seen his mother use salve all the time to cure runny noses, aching joints and muscles, and for a lot of other things, too. If she used salve, then probably everyone in Bloomington used salve. He could make a fortune selling this stuff! So, he ordered a starter supply of salve. The company would send it to him with instructions on how to sell, collect and earn his commissions. He waited impatiently for the shipment to arrive. Young Snook had many admirable qualities; however, patience was not among them. It was never part of Q.L.'s "schedule." Nor would it ever be. He was forever in a hurry to advance his "schedule" of things to accomplish. He disliked waiting on anyone who had become a part of that schedule.

When the salve finally arrived, Quentin triumphantly packed it up, walked the four miles into Bloomington and began going door to door. He picked out the large brick houses, reasoning to himself that these homeowners certainly had enough money to buy his salve. It never even crossed his mind that people wouldn't buy his salve. After all, everyone used salve! All that day he knocked on doors and presented his salve from the Attica Salve Company. He had big plans for the commissions he would earn! But it wasn't to be. Without exception, he was turned down! It seemed like he'd made a hundred house-to-house calls, and no one bought a single can of salve! The closest he got to a sale was a kindly looking lady who smiled at him and told him that she didn't have any change at that moment, only a dollar bill. She gently explained, "It would be a shame to break a dollar bill for a twenty-five cent can of salve." Q.L. agreed! It would be a shame. He didn't get that sale, either!

Quentin had been so intent on making calls that he had gotten lost and wasn't sure of his way home. As darkness began to set in he reasoned that the streetcar tracks should lead out of town. He followed them until he found a familiar road, and late in the evening, tired and discouraged, he finally made it home.

From his experience with the Attica Salve Company, Q.L. learned early that although no gain came without hard work and considerable sacrifice, it wasn't hard work alone that would get him ahead in life. Every housewife in Illinois used salve, it was true, but his product was more expensive than the common, everyday brand of salve that people in Bloomington used and bought at the pharmacy. He hadn't thought it out. He hadn't done his homework. He had believed the sales pitch in the ad and not listened to his own common sense. He had to hear it from several hundred ladies in a humbling way for several days of hard work!

He learned that hard work was important to earning anything in life, but it needed to be intelligent, planned, and well-researched to bring success. He also learned that to get ahead, there needed to be "extra work." Work above and beyond the necessary task and primary focus of working for the family. From his experiences of watching his mother and father work to care for their family, Q.L. never questioned the primary purpose of his life—work to care for his family. But he also learned that extra work, smarter work, planned and intelligent work could bring extra reward. His experience with Attica Salve and similar work experiences as a boy drove that message home. If he were ever to become wealthy, he'd have to work harder than anyone else.

For all his efforts, young Snook still didn't have that coveted bicycle. He had to find a way to get it.

"My dad didn't say much else about the bicycle, but one day he dropped a little hint that if I still wanted that bicycle, that maybe I could convince my mother to take a few extra vegetables from the garden and open up a stand alongside the road that led to town." Quentin's father suggested that he could add on to the garden space if he cared for it. He'd have to tend the garden himself, however, and expect no help. "Boy, what an idea! I'd go into business!"

That's the way it was for Quentin Snook growing up. The lives of his parents were spent caring for their family. They spared no sacrifice in doing so, often working two jobs and countless hours. They could afford no indulgences: only to keep food on the table and the roof repaired over their heads.

Snook saw it all around him as he grew up in the Depression. He saw the benefits of hard work and the stark reality of the result of not working hard, or having no work. Over the dinner table, Snook would hear his father talk about another neighbor who had just lost their farm, or that another business in town had failed. His dad would shake his head, lead the family in saying grace and become more determined than ever to stay clear of the bread lines. They would survive. They had to. Young Snook listened and learned. He, too, would help his parents. They all would need to do their part.

It was always a thrill for this determined, ambitious boy to see the big black cars rumbling past his house during the hot summer months in Illinois. He wondered who was inside, and where they were going. He'd have a car like that one day. He wouldn't be poor. No, sir. He'd work as hard as it took.

With his father's help, Q.L. built his roadside fruit and vegetable stand. It was his first attempt at business and he liked the challenge of it. He stocked the stand with the finest cucumbers, tomatoes, radishes, muskmelon, watermelon, and corn that the garden had—all compliments of his mother, of course. When apples were in season, they were displayed at the farm stand, too; apples and pears, everything edible and marketable that he could find around his rural home.

He'd run home from school, down the road, do his chores as fast as possible and then work the vegetable stand. On weekends, he had more time, and he'd catch what traffic there was as folks went out for Sunday drives or weekend jaunts.

He learned that it wasn't enough to open the stand and stock it. Cars would motor right past him, not even aware that his stand existed, until it was too late and they were by him. That's how he learned his first lesson about advertising. "You gotta tell people you're open."

"I was in such a hurry to get that sign up hung on a large maple tree, that I spelled cucumbers wrong," Snook recalled with a smile. "I spelled it out: c-u-m-c-u-m-b-e-r-s! CUMCUMBERS! Well, it was an honest mistake!"

But to his amazement, people responded to the misspelling! They would drive up, stop, and get out of their cars smiling, pointing up at the sign. "You misspelled cucumbers," people would say, laughing. "My first inclination was to take it down and fix it, but then I thought to myself: that's one reason people are stopping!"

Innovative advertising. Innovative selling. That simple mistake taught Q.L. something about people: when and what they buy and why. He also learned early on that humor sells.

Q.L. sold a lot of vegetables and fruit at his stand. Every summer he had it open, and people came to rely on him for the best fresh vegetables in the area. Not to mention the price. Young Snook had taken the time to do his homework. He knew what vegetables were selling for in the local market, and he underpriced them. Fresh from the garden, at a better price. His roadside vegetable stand business flourished.

One summer, area crops didn't get into the ground until early July due to bad weather. Q.L. had managed, however, to plant sweet corn earlier. He approached the local Piggly Wiggly food store when his corn matured and they bought all that he had!

With the proceeds of the corn sale, Snook got his bicycle: a red one, brand new. His father helped him pick it out and together they proudly brought it home. Without the willingness to plant plenty of sweet corn when others couldn't, Snook wouldn't have had his bicycle. He took a chance and it paid off handsomely. He had capitalized on the bad weather and brought sweet corn to a hungry and eager market. That lesson would not be forgotten.

During the summer months of his high school years, Q.L. worked for Johnny O'Neil, a German fruit and vegetable vendor. O'Neil lived a mile west of the Snook home and drove a four-wheel wagon with a roof cover, drawn with a horse. Mr. O'Neil and Q.L. would make calls on customers in Bloomington. This block-by-block selling of their fruit and vegetables began before daylight and continued until dark. For his efforts assisting Mr. O'Neil, Q.L. received thirty-five cents for the day! He was always glad to get it!

It wasn't just in his first business that young Snook put forth a great effort. Working hard came natural to him. It was the fastest way to achieve whatever goal that he had created for himself. In school, he learned that it was the fastest way to complete his studies. If he studied hard the first time, he didn't have to make up any bad work or have to repeat a class, like some others in the class had to do.

He learned that there were few shortcuts to working hard. It was the fastest way to get the morning and evening chores done, the fastest way to get his homework done, the fastest way to earn extra money. It was clear to him. Why do it any other way?

We do it all for our family

In Snook's family, as in so many during the Great Depression, survival for the family meant that everyone, young and old alike, worked at keeping the family fed, safe, sheltered, clothed and educated. It wasn't a topic for discussion or debate. No one in the family questioned their need to contribute. There were many days he didn't feel like cleaning out the stove after school and refilling the coal bucket, feeding chickens and rabbits, but he wouldn't ever be accused of not carrying his load in the family. That just wasn't done then, nor was it done later in his life. He saw the daily sacrifices of his mother and father. They put their children's needs first, each other's second and their own needs and desires, dead last. It was the same for his brothers, Morris, Wilbur and Herbert, and for his sisters, Shirley, Ruth and Esther. The girls helped cook, clean and care for the house. The boys did the outside work and helped their dad. Later, when Q.L.'s father started a portable feed mill, they all headed for the mill as soon as the school bell rang. Their father needed their help, and all four of the Snook boys with three girls were called upon to do their part.

Q.L.'s siblings have gone their separate ways over the years as all family members inevitably do.

Clayton Morris, Jr. died in 1958. Wilbur died is 1985. Shirley Hinthorn retired after twenty-two years as a secretary on the staff of St. Joseph Medical Center. She and Vernon are living in Bloomington, Ill. Ruth

Marian retired as a health professional and lives in Bloomington with her husband Bill McGath. Esther retired as a health professional and lives in Phoenix, Arizona with her husband J. Robert Shinn. Herbert retired as a teacher and works in real estate. He and his wife Ethel live in Portland, Oregon.

"Roles were different then," Snook reasons. "My father never questioned his responsibility to us all. I never heard him complain. He would work whatever hours it took, and we would help him. It was the same for my mother and sisters. No one shirked their responsibilities around the house, and if anyone of us tried, we quickly learned it wasn't tolerated. It wasn't the whipping I feared, it was the disappointment in my mother's eyes."

Q.L. later had five children of his own, and he witnessed the changing roles of men, women and children through his own kids. Different generations had completely changed what he had been taught. Right or wrong, for better or worse, the changing roles have caused confusion, divorce and family trouble. The family structure that had been so important when he was growing up, had changed. Parents disciplined their children to teach them right from wrong. Children helped their parents so that everyone could eat, keep the roof from leaking, and be able to afford the few luxuries they could manage. Mothers wouldn't dream of aborting an unborn child. It seemed to Snook that life was simpler then, with fewer choices. In Snook's opinion, perhaps that was good.

"When I got married, I naturally stepped into the same role my father had taught me so well. A man has to care for his wife and children. There isn't any need to discuss any other schedule. I had to put a roof over our heads, so I built my first house. It was at 307 Ells Avenue in Champaign. It didn't have plumbing for the entire first year we lived there. The plumber couldn't secure the soil pipe needed to make a final connection for bath and kitchen waste. None of the soil pipe was available due to the war." With no facilities, the young married couple had to walk to their neighbors, Richard and Lois Meyer at 412 Ells Avenue. Snook had been a renter of the Meyers earlier when he was a student.

"But I had gotten on with my plan, my goal. I wanted extra, so I naturally knew that I would have to work extra. My first goal was to earn five years of pay in three."

For Snook and so many of that Depression generation, the roles of men, women and children were clearly defined. However, he saw all of that change.

"I think that before my sons got married, they were looking for someone like their mother. I know I was, before I got married. But women want more now. They want to have careers and independence."

Snook believes that it is these changing roles, discovered by both women and men, that have put the family in flux and turmoil. The old formula of children first, each other second and yourself, dead last, seems to have changed, almost reversed.

"For some, it is placing ourselves first in the equation. Today, some ask, 'What's in it for me? What can bring me satisfaction?' Somewhere further down the list of priorities come your spouse and children."

Because of those role changes, the focus of work has also changed. While saving money was a precious necessity in the tough times of the Depression, it became passe in the generation that followed. There seemed to be an abundance of money then. While debt was a millstone to avoid at all costs when he grew up, it became an accepted standard as time went on. The stigma of owing money somehow became commonplace. It had all changed.

"The focus of work should be on your family," Q.L. believes. "If it isn't, the family may start to suffer from other personal indulgences. Those should be avoided at any price," he advises.

"Every problem has a solution," Snook is fond of saying. "Whether in business or in family matters, if you focus on the solution, and not the problem, you can resolve any problem. Whether you are faced with stiff competition in business or deep debt in your personal life, get off the problem, and get started on solutions. That is where your thinking needs to be."

Family has been the motivator in Snook's life just as it was for his father. He has lived with the philosophy taught to him by his mother and father: "Work hard, work smart, work for your family. Avoid personal indulgences. They all come at the expense of your family."

When his father died at the age of sixty-three in an accident at the Snook Feed Mill in Bloomington, Quentin was devastated. Clayton Snook had been his idol, his mentor. No one would ever have as much of an effect or influence on Quentin as his father. No one would ever be loved as much by him, either. His father's philosophy had been sound and kind, and his wisdom acquired by the hardships and experiences in his life.

"When you have lost everything you have, or thought you had, you reevaluate your priorities," Snook believes. "It always comes back to your family. Businesses can be gained or lost. Money can be earned or squandered, but your family is forever."

I just knew that I never wanted to be poor

Just down the road from the Snook house in Bloomington was the McLean County Poor Farm, a place where individuals who were in need of help were sent to live. As a young boy Snook saw many people heading down that road. The Depression was hard on every family, but due to fierce pride, no one ever wanted to admit they couldn't care for their family or themselves. "On the dole" was not a place anyone wanted to be.

Snook also remembers transients who would come by the house looking for a handout, a day's work, or a free meal. These transients would often mark a tree alongside the road where others might recognize that this was a house where they could get a meal.

"I remember one afternoon we got a knock on the front door. I'm not sure where my brothers and sisters were, but I think I was alone with my mother. I ran to the door and behind the screen I saw a man with a beard wearing tattered and dirty clothes. His face was flushed from the summer heat. He greeted me with a smile and asked if the 'master of the house' was in. I retreated and made way for my mother.

"We didn't fear strangers in those days. We rarely ever locked our doors. My mother showed no signs of fear toward the haggard-looking man. He talked with her quietly and she invited him to rest on our steps while she went back into the kitchen and fixed him a meal and poured him a cold glass of water. I sat on the steps outside with him and watched him eat, barely able to take my eyes off of him. Where had he come from? Where was he going? He looked like he hadn't eaten in a month of Sundays.

"Without a lot of conversation my mother made him wash his hands and fed him, right then and there. When he finished she refilled his plate and poured him another glass of water. The man ate quietly, occasionally glancing at me staring at him. He smiled softly and continued eating. When he finally finished his meal he offered to work, but my mother refused his offer. Then he reached into his deep pocket and took out the only thing he had in it. It was a nickel.

" 'Let me at least pay you what I can,' he said, and offered me the nickel. I remember looking at that dirty buffalo head and thinking to myself, 'wow, a nickel!' I turned the coin over in my hand, much to the old fellow's delight, and was about to pocket that nickel when my mother told me to return it to him. Without another thought about it, I stuck out my little hand and offered it back. Putting his hat back on, the hobo picked the nickel from my palm and departed."

"God bless you, ma'am. An' you too, boy." With that, he disappeared down the lane from the front yard.

Poverty was all around the Snook family. America was in the midst of a deepening Depression. Farms and businesses were lost every day. Whether the Snook house was "ribboned" and targeted by the transients of the Midwest, Q.L. never knew, but his mother always fed anyone who asked for and needed a meal. The image of that red-brick county poor farm, and the image of unfortunate transients who had nowhere to live and nowhere to go, never left him. Q.L. knew he wanted to be a responsible citizen.

The Depression illustrated the fine line between riches and poverty. For most of those families who barely survived the crash of businesses and the country's economy, the line was even thinner. A few days after a layoff, maybe a few weeks, and a family could be destitute, often with little hope of recovery.

The tragedy of sudden economic loss might have been something to happen only to those other than young Snook. After all, Quentin was only a boy. But the full impact of the era was to come right up and smack him as well.

Q.L. had learned at a young age to be thrifty. He learned it from his mother and father. They, too, were frugal. Economizing was not an option for most families; it was a necessity. So, having been taught from an early age to save any extra money he could earn, he opened a savings account at the Liberty State Bank in Bloomington. He would often look at the entries in the passbook. His name was on it, along with his father's. That made Q.L. feel quite important. Eventually, the account grew to a sizeable sum for a young boy who could save only pennies and nickels at a time. Therefore, he was extremely proud of his savings account. It gave him some distance from the man who had only a nickel to his name.

So when the bank closed one morning and he lost his savings account, he was bitterly disappointed. "When my dad told me the bank went out of business, I couldn't believe it! How was I going to get my money? When would I get it back? I suppose my dad knew I'd never get it back, but he didn't tell me that. People with large or small savings were in the same situation. Everyone lost. I never trusted a bank again. Even though I know they are insured, I was given back three dollars and thirteen cents! That's all the money they could give me. To this day I keep very little money in any bank. It isn't the place to put money away."

Although the Depression had the same effect on most people of the time, Snook would never forget the "meagerness" of the times. While his family was more fortunate than many, they were by no means "well off." He silently vowed he would never be without. He also vowed that no bank would break him again. He made plans, set goals and began a schedule that eventually would lead him to wealth. The lessons of the time were too painful for anything else. As though driven by the ghosts of the red-brick poor farm, Snook promised himself that, at any cost, he would succeed. He wouldn't go without. He would never forget the deep, sorrowful eyes of that hobo on the steps outside their house and the offering he had made for a meal. Q.L. vowed that would never happen to him.

In later years, Q.L., at the age of twenty-five, fresh from college and the military, with his bride in hand, opened his business, Q.L. Snook Construction Company, from the back of his house. For himself, he established two goals. The first was to earn five years' worth of income in three years and to save at least twenty percent of it. The second was far more reaching. A "pipe dream" maybe, nevertheless Q.L. vowed to himself that he would work and work, and he would be financially independent in ten years. A fantasy of a young, new entrepreneur in Champaign, Illinois? Perhaps.

Waste not, want not

Life during the Depression was a great struggle to survive for families. Economizing became a way of life that everyone accepted, whether they wanted to or not. Adopted from earlier generations when pioneer families first settled the land, successful depression-era families lived by the motto "waste not, want not."

For a young boy growing up in the thirties, Quentin simply adopted this philosophy. Frugality was a way of life, and became for many, an internal source of pride. Little or nothing was wasted. In Snook's family, it was his mother who laid down the law of frugality.

"When my mother cooked, she made large quantities of food. We ate leftovers all the time. If a small quantity of corn was left over, she saved it and made soup with a ham or beef bone. As I recall, she didn't throw away anything that was edible, ever. What we could burn in our stove, we did. Coal cost money. We used it only when we needed it."

Even at school, young Snook learned the basics of economizing.

"The Houghton School was about a half a mile down the road. It was a two-room, rural school that had eight grades. During those elementary school years my teachers were a husband and wife team named Mr. and Mrs. Dewey Fristoe. We used our lead pencils until we could hardly hold them anymore, writing with them right down to small nubs! But I particularly remember one day that Mr. Fristoe took us boys into the washroom, showing us how to use only one paper towel to dry our hands. Meticulously, he showed us how to wring the excess water off our hands after we washed and then carefully use that single sheet of paper towel to completely dry our hands. I never forgot it, and do it to this day!" Years later, in a washroom in Deltona, Snook witnessed a young boy wasting five or six sheets of paper hand towels. He could have observed him saying nothing, but he didn't. Much to the boy's chagrin, Snook commented about the waste and showed him the trick of using only one towel.

It is Snook's belief that being frugal is not only a way to save money and build wealth, it is also a way of life that others could adopt as well.

"My mother would roll over in her grave if she saw how much food we, as a society, throw away today. But it isn't just food; it's everything. We wear a hole in our jeans or the soles of our shoes and we want to throw them away! What's the matter with a patch or a set of new soles? Still plenty of wear in them." Q.L. and Margaret Snook take pride in being frugal and living modestly.

"The way to build wealth is to learn to live on less. You don't have to deprive yourself of anything, just don't waste money on foolish things."

Snook's examples of extravagance could make up a long list, including going out to the movies. He adamantly believes that, with all the movies on television, why pay for one? Although others may view this as somewhat fanatical, this belief is simply another carryover from his childhood.

"I can remember going to one of the first movies I ever saw. I paid my nickel, or whatever it was, and sat and watched that whole movie. After it ended I stayed seated and watched it all over again. No one asked me to leave and I thought that for five cents I might as well see it twice. It seemed to be a better value for my money."

When it came to money, Snook was a natural saver. That also was a lesson of the times he grew up in.

"If I made twenty-five cents at the vegetable stand on a Saturday, my mother would always ask how much of it I was going to put in the bank and save. Usually, it was all of it. I felt good about saving money and knew that I would never be without if I saved. Look at nature; you don't see squirrels going off on their merry way come autumn, do you? They are packing acorns and nuts away for winter as fast as they can. It's natural. It is common sense."

The young married couple vowed to save at least twenty percent of their combined salaries. Margaret was a teacher and Q.L. was setting up his own construction company. Since there was very little property for sale, the couple decided to build their own house. Having little or no money, they applied for a mortgage.

"My dad even cautioned me about borrowing money to build a house. But I knew what I was doing."

After the house was completed, Snook paid a visit to the Citizens Building & Loan to sign the papers for the mortgage. However, after he arrived, the attorney hired to clear the title informed Snook that the loan could not be made because there was a *cloud* on the title.

"Whatever does the weather have to do with anything about my loan?" Snook asked, tongue in cheek.

The attorney informed him that a tax lien of $167 existed on the property. No loan could be granted until it was resolved.

"How can I pay my subcontractors?" Snook argued. "Why hadn't this surfaced before?" Then an idea came to him. What if they subtracted the $167 from the loan and placed it in escrow with the loan company? Wouldn't that solve the problem? "Lawyers aren't the most innovative people in the world sometimes. The loan was granted and all the bills were paid."

After they were able to install plumbing and to help defray the costs, the Snooks took on a renter, Bill Jeffrey, who was looking for housing and exchanged his labor for room rent.

The house was nothing fancy. Even the floors weren't finished. But it was home. The Snooks took on second renters, who were looking for a place to live, Dick and Rene Carlisle.

"We've forgotten about saving money today," Snook says. "Statistics say that it will take a million dollars for a baby boomer couple to retire comfortably. Anything less isn't enough. You ask the average couple about their financial situation and regular saving usually doesn't even enter the picture. If it does, the savings level is way too low."

For Q.L. Snook, the mechanics of earning wealth revolve around some pretty basic principles that anyone can successfully adopt.

- First is a good job, that has good earning capacity.
- Second is hard work at that job, being innovative and supportive of the company's efforts and never shirking your duties at the job.
- Third is regular savings. Twenty percent should be a minimum target goal.
- Fourth is frugal living: not going into debt, avoiding interest payments of any kind, except real estate as home.
- Fifth is allowing your savings to earn extra money and begin to work for you.

"Smart investing is a learned skill. You stay clear of highly speculative endeavors until you can afford to lose all that money! There are much better places to invest money than in banks." These include credit unions and a building and loan association until you can qualify to move into money market funds, mutual funds, stocks, bonds and other investments.

The final money management skill that Snook maintains is vital to building wealth, is a disciplined lifestyle. Taking charge of your actions and anticipating reactions to them. If you are in debt, stop spending. Indulgences are contrary to family values and should be avoided at all costs, whether these indulgences are drinking, smoking, gambling, overeating, or too much recreation. All create risk to harmonious family life, according to Snook.

Waste not, want not, has been a theme of Q.L. Snook's life. "It becomes a game, an enjoyable game," he says. "It feels good to have money saved, the debts of the family paid in full, and some direction for that accumulated money to start working for you."

The driving energy of most successful people is fear of loss

The loss of his money in the Liberty State Bank in 1936 was a painful lesson for young Q.L. Snook. He wouldn't let it happen to him again. It became a powerful motivating force in his business life and one that he believes explains successful people and successful companies all over the world; that is, successful people eventually profit from a loss and don't let others use or cheat them.

"My dad was a kind man, and I remember seeing people use him when he operated the feed mill. People would owe him money and he would make excuses for them. Or they might become demanding and he would allow it. It bothered me to see people take advantage of him."

One such incident occurred at the Snook Feed Mill on a Saturday morning. Q.L. had been bagging ground oats for a customer. Never one to work on just one project at a time, he was also mixing feed in the mixer for another customer, carefully selecting the proper ingredients for the customer's needs.

Unexpectedly, a small amount of dust from the bagging operation was swept into the mixer. The customer saw Q.L. do this and went into a rage, yelling at his father to deduct the dust and residue which the younger Snook had gotten into his mixer. The man yelled at Quentin's father, "I'll put you out of business for this kind of stuff!"

The elder Snook calmed the man and assured him that he would get some credit for Quentin's small error. Still angry, the man huffed off, leaving young Snook at a total loss of words.

"You can't please everyone," my father told me. "You just don't even try, or you'll run from here to there trying to make everyone happy with you." It was another lesson that Q.L. would adopt in his business life as he grew older.

But Q.L. took issue with his father in this incident, believing the huffy customer was wrong and shouldn't have been allowed any discount for the small amount of floor dust. He didn't win the argument that day, but rarely would he lose one again. Snook reasoned that if his father was right and you couldn't please everyone, all of the time, then why even try and be taken advantage of. If the situation clearly puts you in the right, then you have a moral obligation to stand up for what is right and defend yourself, even at the risk of losing that one hot-headed customer.

Honesty and integrity became Q.L. Snook trademarks. He doesn't believe in being anything less than open and honest in all of his dealings. He believes that to be a truly successful person, you have to be an honest person, first and foremost.

"Any shortcut you take, any half-truth or lie you tell, will eventually come back and bite you hard," Snook believes. "If you are honest with your customers, your employees, your family and friends, you will be rewarded for that honesty ten-fold. On the other hand, if you live by the half-truths and dishonesty that prevail in a lot of businesses today, you will be discovered, sooner or later, and you and your business will suffer. Honesty makes good business sense."

In addition to honesty in all endeavors, fear of loss is a prime motivator in all circles of life, according to Snook. Whether it is in a high school track meet, a marriage, business dealings or your relationship to God, it all boils down to the fear of losing what is valuable to you. Understanding that fear and turning it into a positive expression is a vital link to successful business and living.

"If you're afraid of losing your job, work harder, volunteer to do something else for the company. Find out a way to increase your value to the company. Make yourself more useful and vital to the company's future. Ask yourself, 'What can I do to make myself more valuable to the company?' It is turning a negative emotion into a positive expression such as finding a solution to a potential problem. Don't focus on the fear of losing your job, focus on the desire to keep your job by working harder, smarter and increasing your value."

"The same is true in your marriage, or with your children, or in your business. The fear of losing valuable time with your children or your spouse can be turned into a positive action of reevaluating priorities and taking the time to spend with family members. But first, you must recognize the fear within you, and understand that there is a logical solution to it."

Another way to lessen the fear of loss is to make sure you've done your homework. When Snook started his construction business in Champaign-Urbana, Illinois, in 1946, he knew there was going to be competition. He studied the competition, studied them in detail. He even went to visit them and asked them about their business! They shared their business philosophy with him without his asking. He was determined that his construction business wouldn't fail. He turned that fear of loss into a positive solution when he studied up on the competition, found their weaknesses and profited by overcoming those weaknesses in the market.

"The biggest contractor in town was building most of the new homes at low prices," Snook recalled. "They undercut everyone and got business that way. But when I analyzed their profitability and their cost of materials, I knew they couldn't hold on for long. They simply weren't building in enough profit. They built cheap and fast."

Snook started his construction company with the building of his own home on Ells Avenue. The care and detail of his building design and methods were quickly noticed by others. A critical shortage of housing following the war, aided him in his building efforts. Snook's efforts to help his renters spread and people began to look to him for assistance on other building projects.

"A customer was looking for a builder living near my home. The customer thought I was that builder. The customer asked me to build a house for him, which I did. One man asked me to consider erecting the shell for a duplex that he was building. Another asked me to pour a foundation.

"People saw the quality with which I was building, and they didn't even talk price. They wanted the quality," Snook recalls.

Snook built his reputation on the fear of losing his quality advantage over his customers. His goals were to have happy and satisfied customers. It became the prime motivation for all the businesses he was to create.

I never wanted to work for someone else

From his earliest memory, Q.L. Snook was persistent. As a boy in rural Illinois Snook rarely accepted help from others if he could avoid it. It seemed to him that he should be able to figure things out for himself.

"When I was learning to ride a bicycle, my dad offered to help me, but I just had to learn on my own. It wouldn't be the same experience if I didn't."

Using the fence that surrounded the Snooks' home for balance, Snook learned to ride. Not the first time, or the second, but he learned, although it took most of the day and a few scrapes to his knees.

This pattern of persistence in his everyday life became a driving force throughout his life. It later blossomed into a fierce need to be independent of outside help. He was determined from an early age to "do it himself." He didn't want to be at the mercy of anyone, but to rely on himself. He established high standards for himself; for example, in his final years of high school, Q.L. took every business course offered, including shorthand. Shorthand was a class dominated by females, but that didn't bother him.

"Shorthand was a faster way to write, and I looked for the fastest way to do everything. The class was full of girls; actually, I was the only boy in there."

But shorthand didn't come easy for him; in fact, he was flunking the class.

"Above the door going into that classroom, there was a saying carved on a wooden board: *It Can Be Done!* I would read that every day I entered that room. It seemed to me that shorthand was a necessity in business and I was going to learn it."

Q.L. took his shorthand book with him everywhere. When he milked the family cow, the shorthand book was open.

"Maybe I figured that if I kept the book with me all the time, I would learn it by osmosis or something," Snook says, laughing. In the end, he passed the shorthand course.

Snook was the first of his family to graduate from college. He enrolled at Illinois Wesleyan University, planning to major in business. His mother had attended school on the IWU campus at Hedding Hall Academy. His uncle, Thomas Maurice, was on the Illinois Wesleyan University football team 1900-1902, while a student.

"My father paid for my first semester. I didn't like that idea, but didn't have any real choice. That was the one time I accepted money from my dad."

Illinois Wesleyan offered Snook a scholarship after his first semester and he took it. He was determined to get through in record time.

"I just had to get on with life," Snook says, fully aware of his long-held obsession with time. "The fastest way to graduate was to take more semester hours. I took all I could and still worked two jobs."

Other events were occurring on a global scene that would delay that decision. The war in Europe was intensifying. News stories kept America informed of how Germany was systematically overrunning Europe. It was the topic of every conversation in every corner of America. Law school in Champaign would have to wait.

Many of Q.L.'s high school and college friends were being drafted. He was feeling the pull of the military more and more, and eventually enrolled in a civilian pilot's training program to learn how to fly. "I guess I figured that if war broke out, the best place for me to be would be in the air, as a pilot."

Although Snook had no prior flying experience, he never doubted he could fly. A famous Snook, Anita, had gained fame years earlier when she instructed a young female pilot. The woman aviator was none other than Amelia Earhart. Never one to avoid a challenge, he took ground school training one night a week and then hitchhiked several miles once a week to the airport for his flying lessons. His mother, Genevieve, was dead set against the idea. She believed that World War I ended war! The war in Europe now worried her.

Snook's love of flying lasted for the rest of his life. He applied the same detailed preparation to flying that he did with everything else in his life. He trained and retrained himself until he was confident of his abilities. He learned early in life to calculate risk, lessening it where he could, but never being afraid of it. He had a few close calls while flying, including an occasion when an engine cut out while flying near Jacksonville, Florida. He never panicked, however, and managed to land safely, knowing that he always had a back-up plan.

Q.L.'s brother, Morris, had enlisted before the December 7, 1941 bombing of Pearl Harbor to serve in the Flying Tigers in Burma. His other brother, Herbert would also be drafted. His sisters Shirley, Esther and Ruth Marian had husbands who would serve in World War II.

Understandably, Genevieve Snook was worried and nervous, with three sons and the husbands of her daughters in the war. All would survive as veterans.

She argued with Q.L. about military service. They disagreed often about his choice. But Snook saw purposes in flying beyond the military. It was a long and arduous task, in addition to everything else he was doing, but he persisted and finally attained his private pilot's license, followed with his commercial license after WWII.

The bombing of Pearl Harbor changed the course of history for Americans, including Snook. Within days of the devastation of the U.S. Naval Fleet in Hawaii, the fever of retribution burned hot in everyone's heart. Most available men dropped what they had been doing and enlisted. Snook was no exception.

"I enlisted in the navy and put in for the flight school," Snook says. "It was an anxious time for everyone." It was September of 1943.

But the years of lifting feed sacks with his father at the mill had taken an unexpected toll on young Snook's body. With little prior knowledge of it, he had damaged his back and soon greatly aggravated it in naval training. The pain increased. Not wanting to complain, he persisted, but eventually the pain drove him to the infirmary.

A year had passed, however, before the diagnosis had been made—a year of Snook's life that delayed his efforts to amass a fortune. The war in Europe, or in the Pacific, wouldn't be Snook's calling, whether he wished for it or not. He was given a convenience discharge.

Getting back to his routine was difficult though. Friends of his from Illinois Wesleyan were enlisting and heading overseas. Some didn't return. Snook tried to regain his drive for law school, but once again his plans would be postponed. With a convenience discharge from the navy, Snook wouldn't understand what would come next.

"I couldn't believe it when I opened the mail one afternoon and there were draft orders for the army!" Snook exclaims. "I had been discharged from the navy and now was getting drafted into the army!"

He responded to the draft notice, telling the draft board he had already been discharged. They didn't listen. Somehow he passed his physical and was sent to basic training at Fort Knox. Although he was a licensed pilot, the army sent him for training in the artillery.

His orders assigned him to Korea. The rigorous army basic training caused recurring back pain.

He was in such pain that the only way he could sleep was to lie flat on his stomach on the floor to get some relief. The training was killing him, but he never complained.

After army training Snook was sent for his overseas physical. This time, the army doctor took more time. Just as Snook thought that Korea might be in his future, his hopes were dashed again. The doctor told Snook that he wouldn't be going anywhere. In fact, he released Snook from active duty to give him a medical discharge with a forty percent disability from the army.

"From then on, I was in a powerful hurry. I had to make up for the lost time."

He was accepted into the University of Illinois Law School and enrolled as soon as he could.

"Law school was tougher than I expected," Snook said of those first semesters. "I worked and worked and worked at it, but the grades weren't coming. I had too many other distractions in my life then."

With mediocre grades due to the rigorous schedule of work and law classes, he was warned to get his grades up. Determined to make it, he worked all the harder. But he was finding that the study of law was too confining and restrictive. His scope and the interests in business around him were widening.

*****

It has been said that the highest honor a man can boast of is the number of friends that he can count. Those friends, far too numerous to mention, have volunteered to share their feelings for Quentin Laurence Snook.

To know Q.L. Snook is one great experience in a lifetime you never forget. We all tend to want to be like him for several reasons. He wants to know "what's next." Unsurpassed energy and so correct. I am sure one of these days he will want to arrange his own funeral and probably raise up from his coffin and say "Let's go on with this!" Or, he may get impatient and just fly away, for he knows the way. And, he will fly first class, because he knows the CAPTAIN. That's Q.L. Snook, always buoyant with his eyes straight ahead.

Weston Covington, Retired Real Estate Broker, San Diego, California

I've known Q.L. Snook for over eight years. His interest and efforts in helping others rank him among the finest people I've known. His intelligence, dynamic personality and love of entrepreneurship put him among the leaders of our community. The world needs more people like Q.L. Snook!

Edward Ogen, Champaign, Illinois

Quentin and I were close friends in high school. After graduation I moved to Chicago. Although we drifted apart as a lot of high school friends do, I often thought of him. I

41

am proud to have known him and proud also of his many achievements in the business world. I wish him continued good health and happiness. Quentin will always remain a close friend.

Orville Mohr, Bloomington, Illinois

My friendship with Q.L. has certainly been interesting if not a little intriguing. As I am a local in this vicinity, I have always heard of Q.L. Snook. Most of the information related to an insurance business and was all positive. Then, in 1986, I moved to a residence that was just a few houses from his home. In a short time we became friends and to this day maintain a close personal relationship. Many times we have had the opportunity to sit and discuss a myriad of topics and I find it to be very interesting and fulfilling. I admire Q.L.'s work ethic and firmly believe that he has the energy for any task that he sets forth to complete. The man is always busy! I am intrigued with the fact that he accepts and respects individuals with a trust that is foreign to this day and age. He has allowed me and others to frequent his home during his absence with the utmost assurance of safety. I am honored to know Q.L., one who still has confidence in mankind.

Gerald A. Morgan, Supervisor,
University of Illinois Police Dept., Savoy, Illinois

2 GATHERING TOOLS FOR SUCCESS

Learn to listen and listen to learn

Being open and receptive for opportunity when it comes knocking is a key to success, according to Snook. In his life, he refers to the many "accidents" that occurred to him. "Accidently" being in the right spot at the right time is serendipitous, and Q.L. recalls that on several occasions, his life has been influenced by such serendipity. He also calls it "psychic income" and providence. He feels that we all have those opportunities that pass in front of us, and it is our choice whether we choose to reach out for them or not.

Snook refers to this process as *active listening.* In his own life, he has learned to listen closely to that thoroughfare of opportunity that runs by us all. It involves a process of not getting so involved in our day-to-day activities that we fail to listen, and then, listen to learn. People who know Q.L. Snook might say that he seems to be *occupied with his thoughts* from time to time. Intensely listening for those morsels of *psychic income* to confront him, Snook maintains that this phenomenon has happened to him since birth. He learned that preparation plus opportunity can lead to greater success.

"I was planting a garden in the backyard at our first house in Champaign," Snook recalls. "I was working three jobs and was busy planting this garden so that we could save a little money on fresh vegetables. I had a schedule for everything, and didn't waste one minute of time! I had a snap-on watch and slip-in shoes so I could get right to things."

On one particular Saturday afternoon, Snook busied himself hoeing in the garden when Margaret informed him that he had a visitor at the front door.

"Well, I didn't have any time to see that person, and told Margaret so. I didn't let anyone break into my schedule."

But his wife insisted that maybe he should see this man. Finally he agreed. He recalled being irritated by the interruption and kept on hoeing in the garden. He'd see the man, but he wouldn't stop work! Margaret led the man through the house, out the back door and right to where Snook was hoeing. They waited for him to break, but he didn't.

"When he saw I wasn't going to quit, he finally introduced himself and said he was Frank Bertram, with Kansas City Life Insurance Company. I couldn't believe that Margaret had led a salesman through the house, into the backyard, and now he stood in my garden!"

But the man didn't ask Q.L. to buy life insurance, although that may have been his motive. He asked Q.L. what occupation he was in and if it paid him what he wanted to make. That got Snook's attention, but he didn't slow down and kept his eyes cast toward the weeds. Then, realizing that this might be one of those moments that *he should listen*, he impatiently answered the salesman.

"No, I don't think any job could pay me what I want to earn."

The salesman smiled and told Q.L. that in insurance he could make up to fifty percent commissions, and that with everyone being a prospective customer, he should consider selling insurance.

Fifty percent commission!

"It hit me like a sack of feed," Snook says of that moment. "I threw down my hoe, stepped out of that garden and invited the man into the house. I kid you not."

That opportunity in the back of his home on Ells Avenue in Champaign would set Q.L. Snook on a new road. It would literally change his life. Although he hadn't planned to listen for opportunity, he did anyway, recognizing the knock at his front door.

Snook took the Kansas City Life Insurance Company's exam for licensing after he set his mind to studying and learning the materials that salesman brought him. Like anything Snook encountered in life, he took it on with vigor and passion. He knew only two speeds, *stop* and *go*. He passed the licensing exam with a very high score. He also completed courses at Illinois Wesleyan in life insurance and actuarial science. He was given his license and a territory in Champaign in which to sell.

The company sent an experienced salesman to work with Snook. His name was Col. Maurice Smith.

Snook valued Smith's experience and ability to sell life insurance and resolved, once again, to listen and learn.

"Col. Smith gave me leads in my first few weeks," Snook says. "He showed me by example how to approach people, how to present the policy and its benefits and how to close the sale. I learned more from that man than I could have ever imagined. I listened and learned."

Snook recalls his first sale. The client was a younger man, and Col. Smith had advised Q.L. of the strategy he was going to need to sell this man. "Younger people can be hard to sell because they haven't thought much about insurance and the benefits of insurance at their age."

The two men came to call on the client and Q.L. observed and listened, as he was instructed to do. "Col. Smith convinced that man so thoroughly of his need to buy that policy that the sale was over before I knew he was trying to sell him anything! He wanted that policy so bad that he asked if we would *take a note to pay for it!*"

Snook would go on to set sales records for Kansas City Life Insurance Company. He would stay with them for four years. Q.L. later joined Land of Lincoln Life Insurance Company and advanced to become the vice president of the company. He would become a regional director of Republic Investors Life Insurance Company, and he would eventually create Thomas Jefferson Life Insurance Company. But with all of his success in insurance, Snook recognized that first *he had to be sold on the benefits of life insurance himself.* Once sold on the benefits, he had to learn the best ways to present it and sell it. Then, he says, "The rest was easy."

From childhood, Snook was an observer and a listener to anyone that he thought had something to say. As a boy he listened and observed his father, and learned from the moral code of ethics which his mother and father lived by. He listened and was eager to learn everything he could. He learned to sell life insurance and became one of the best in the business, *perhaps accidentally,* because he listened to and learned from the best. He learned also to listen to his wife, Margaret, when she insisted upon him seeing a salesman in the backyard and *a thousand other times in his life,* when he had become preoccupied with some activity.

For Snook, an effective tool for success is listening. Education is good, experience is good, proper capital and other management tools are necessary, but nothing takes the place of learning to listen, and listening to learn.

The role of providence

You don't have to talk to Q.L. Snook long before you hear him say, "It just makes good sense." It doesn't matter what subject matter you are talking about, either. Whether it is complicated investment strategies, employee hiring, a tough decision for the board of directors, or dealing with his children, Snook has lived by an internal compass, which he maintains everyone has, and everyone should learn to trust.

"My father wouldn't tell me to do this or to do that, when I was growing up," Snook recalls. "He would usually ask me a question back when I asked him something." As a boy it used to irritate him sometimes. He was looking for an answer, but his dad usually dealt with it by asking a probing question in return. Q.L. would eventually see the wisdom in that, as well as the wisdom of answering the question yourself, using that internal instrument called common sense.

"I can recall asking my dad if it would be all right for me not to go to high school," Snook says, laughing. "I really thought high school would be a waste of time. I could accomplish so much if I worked and got on with my life." As was his custom, Clayton Snook pondered the thought for a moment and asked his son if he thought there was anything to learn in high school? The conversation went on for a while, with the younger Snook giving a grandiose recital for his argument against attending high school. When finally

50

his dad asked, "Do you want to work at the feed mill the rest of your life?" in a kind manner, the conversation ended as abruptly as it had begun!

Snook felt strongly that he had been cheated out of two years of his life due to the two brief encounters with the military. Although painful, Q.L. tried his hardest not to let lower back pain hamper his early efforts in business. Pain or no pain, he felt that he had to make up for lost time.

But his lower back wasn't Snook's only medical malady. He suffered greatly from symptoms of cold, too.

"All day long my nose would run. I'd get multiple sneezing fits. My eyes watered. I was just miserable and it wasn't getting better." He saw several doctors and was irritated that they couldn't solve the problem.

In desperation, Snook decided on a bold move. He talked it over with Margaret, his young wife who was mother of their two sons, and they decided that perhaps a move to Florida might provide the relief he so desperately sought. No medication he had taken offered any relief from the constant sniffling and wheezing. He struck out to find gainful employment and a place to live in St. Petersburg, Florida.

As a young teacher at Illinois Commercial College, Snook planned to apply to St. Petersburg Community College and settle down with his family. He looked at real estate on his trip south and put a down payment on a lot in St. Petersburg on which to build. In fact, the house was built in just two and one-half months. The Snooks have built many homes they have lived in.

It would start a love affair with Florida that resulted in dual residence between Illinois and Florida since 1951.

Upon the advice of a friend, Snook learned of a young doctor in Champaign. It seemed to Q.L. worth paying him a visit. What could he lose?

"I walked into that young doctor's office with an attitude that there wasn't anything he could do for me," Snook recalls. "I told him that I hated being a slave to a doctor. My life was being made miserable."

The physician's name was Payne, and he would improve Q.L.'s life forever in the next few days. Dr. Payne put Snook on a special diet, avoiding three basic food groups. In the next few weeks, they adjusted the diet, trying different foods and portions of them.

"In three days I was a new man!" Snook exclaims. "I kid you not! It was food allergies the whole time. I avoid any food that gives me cold symptoms!"

Q.L. decided to remain in the Champaign area and build his career. He describes that decision to stay in Champaign as one of the best he has ever made.

He controls his allergies. Snook's back continued to bother him in his early days of building houses and garages, as would be expected. He would work throughout the day and then have to lie flat on the floor for any measurable relief, often for hours.

Snook became a member of the Christian Science Church while in high school. One of the basic philosophies of the church was that through prayer, diet and proper living, the body could heal itself from any malady. Snook decided that if science couldn't help his ailing condition, perhaps religion might. A firm believer as he was growing up, Snook had strayed a bit from the church as he grew into manhood. He had a busy lifestyle, although Snook's absence from Sunday morning church never daunted his belief in the Creator and His master plan for life. It was the lifestyle of most of the people who professed belief in church and its principles and then lived in some other manner, that ultimately bothered him. He also didn't care for the way the church hounded him regularly for money. When they dropped him from the rolls because he hadn't been a regular contributor, he grew distant, if not angry.

But his faith was unwavering. It had been instilled at a young age by the example of his mother and father, and years of going to church, being schooled at church and prayer. While it would be years before Snook and his family attended any church regularly, he would later get involved, and became a generous benefactor of several churches, not just with money, but with his time and great energy.

Q.L. Snook believes to this day that his chronic back pain was healed through a Christian Science healing. He offers no explanation, and few details, but through diligent prayer, and belief, his back pain began to subside, and finally, has all but disappeared in recent years.

With maladies of back pain and allergies in his past, along with the loss of precious time in military service, Q.L. settled upon his plan and hungrily struck out to make his fortune. He had been granted some health pardons, and although he never asked for or wanted them, he would take advantage of the pardons. His goal was to cram five years of work into three. As a young contractor, a part-time college teacher, and then a novice insurance agent, Q.L. Snook was well on his way to being a success.

Be determined

A strong will was something Q.L. Snook was no doubt born with, but it became better and better defined as he grew older. Snook developed the attitude that a strongly determined mind maintains that there is no situation that will be allowed to set you back for long, if at all. He grew fiercely determined to do things himself to gain independence from health maladies, financial distress and mediocrity.

"I saw people take advantage of my dad," Snook cites. "I just couldn't let that happen to me. I was going to the top and no one was going to slow me down."

Working three jobs, Snook excelled in all of them, mainly through hard work, determination and a workable plan. He wasted no time. He couldn't allow it.

"I had a snap-on watch and slip-in shoes," Snook is fond of saying about his early years in business in Champaign. He took in boarders in his first house on Ells Avenue, and they helped pay his mortgage. He began constructing model homes and garages, built by Sears from their plant in Cairo in southern Illinois. Every one he built had already been purchased. He didn't speculate. He couldn't afford to.

Snook's strongest building competitor was a long-time contractor in Champaign who specialized in building quickly and inexpensively. Q.L. took it upon himself to learn all that he could from this established builder, a friend as well as a rival in business. What he

55

didn't know in the building trade he learned. He had great coaches, like his father, and cousin, Hartwell Howard. Howard had made a fortune in real estate and had taken a liking to Snook because of his hunger for success in construction.

"Hartwell taught me a lot about building. He was a giant of a man in my life."

As a self-made man, Hartwell Howard became a role model for Snook to emulate. He was well respected and known as a giver and benefactor to the community. It was far more than building that Snook learned from this distant family relative and close friend. It was a way of life that Q.L. wished to live.

Upon Hartwell's advice, Snook stayed with quality construction instead of trying to compete for pricing. Although he lost jobs to the competitor because of price, his reputation for quality and innovation as a builder began to grow. He also looked for a stronger edge on the competition.

Snook had learned to fly while in college and in preparation for the military. It had become a hobby that he enjoyed very much, but now he saw a practical purpose for his hobby. He pooled his savings to buy a used airplane in 1953 from Lynne Meyer, a local experienced pilot. It would be the first of five planes that Snook would own, each being traded for another in later years.

Not only was Snook's plane an immense symbol of status to his prospective customers, it was purchased for a utilitarian reason. Snook took his innovative ideas about market share to a new level when he began to fly his prospective construction clients to the Sears plant in Cairo so they could see how these modular homes and garages were being built. The concept was innovative for the time: pre-cut houses called *Stylecraft Homes* by the most respected name in the business, Sears.

Snook applied for and was granted the distributorship in the Champaign area for *Stylecraft Homes*. He would board a husband and wife; and, at no charge, fly them to Cairo. The inspection and tour impressed everyone, not to mention the flight, as most of his clients had never been on an airplane!

While at the plant, the customers were treated like royalty. They saw the preconstruction of their home first-hand, every step of the way. The tour included a hands-on inspection of materials, and different stages of development. Snook quietly walked along with them, letting the Cairo plant supervisors do his selling. Once back on his plane and headed for Champaign-Urbana, the couple was already sold.

The construction of modular homes was a new concept in the home building industry. It was typical for Q.L. Snook to be somewhere close to the latest innovation and idea of whatever industry he would become involved with. He was determined that if he couldn't beat the competition's price, he'd win over his customers with service and quality. It was a strategy that worked, and one that worked exceedingly well.

"I started building one house, and then another. No sooner had I gotten that foundation poured and I'd get another going. Business was booming. I carved my niche in the construction market with those *Stylecraft Homes.*"

Snook added construction crews and worked every hour available to him. As fiscally conservative as he was, he never even had an office, but worked from a small space in his home on Ells Avenue, where the mortgage was being paid by his renters.

He had a unique philosophy as it related to his subcontractors. He *overpaid them!* By paying them more than they could earn at his strongest competitor's company, Snook was able to entice the best subcontractors in the area to work for him. He personally supervised every job, and often would add custom features to the home that suited the individual tastes of his customers.

Snook also hired many persons displaced by World War II, who were treated like outsiders by many. Although they often couldn't speak English, Q.L. remembers that they were hard workers doing good work. They worked to pay off passage to America and were grateful for his employment of them.

"You have to give service, the best service you can to your customers. That is the place to start in business. The customer has to feel good about giving you their hard-earned money."

And feel good they did. Snook Construction Company grew from a handful of jobs to one of the best residential construction companies in Champaign. It helped, of course, that the area of Champaign-Urbana was growing by leaps and bounds. His move to this area from nearby Bloomington had been a carefully calculated one. Snook rarely did anything, without careful, conservative and planned deliberation. He believed that if he were to succeed in his endeavor, he needed to be in the right place. Champaign-Urbana was a good choice.

In addition to his booming construction company, Snook was selling insurance at night, and whenever he could arrange appointments during the day. Additionally, he taught business classes from 8 a.m.-3 p.m., Monday through Friday, at Illinois Commercial College. He turned down an offer in a college at Decatur, Illinois, for higher salary. He accepted the position at the Colbert family's Illinois Commercial College. He worked all three positions simultaneously, never sacrificing his most basic principle to any of the jobs—always give the customer, or student, the best service you can.

Snook was excelling at the Kansas City Life Insurance Company. So much so that he was noticed by two young entrepreneurs that had recently formed their own company, Land of Lincoln Life Insurance Company. Upon approaching Snook, Q.L. decided that his opportunities might be better with Land of Lincoln, although the company was newer. Within a year, Snook was appointed vice president of Land of Lincoln. He was one of their top producing agents.

"I really believed in life insurance," Snook says. "I believed everyone needed it and should have it. Once I believe in something with all my heart, I sell it with all my heart!"

And sell he did! His first year with Land of Lincoln, Snook became one of the highest selling agents in the company's history! Every client in his construction business became a client in his insurance business! Almost every subcontractor he had working for him purchased an insurance policy from him. Snook wasted no time in his passion for everyone in Champaign-Urbana becoming well-insured. After all, "Everyone needed to be insured properly." He believed it vehemently.

Working three jobs, however, was understandably trying. Few people could ever keep up with him. He spoke fast, walked faster and slept even faster! Q.L. was a man on a mission. He had ten years to succeed! That was his goal and he was well on his way.

Innovation would strike again for Q.L. and lead to the formation of yet another company. His construction business was making a good friend of his in the home insurance business quite a good living. While Q.L. had grown proficient in selling life insurance, he was still passing, by referral, all the home insurance business of his customers to another company agent.

About the same time as that thought was developing, Q.L.'s third son was born and he needed to give up his office space at home for nursery space! It would lead him out of the security and thriftiness of his home-based business into his first office building.

"I got that building on Springfield Avenue by barter," Snook says of his first office building. "I traded a speculative house that I had built for the office building on Springfield Avenue. He wanted mine and I wanted his." That move was "vintage" Snook.

With expanded quarters, Snook hired his secretary, Nora Witt. She was as capable as anyone Snook could find, and understood his drive, zeal and unusual work habits. Mrs. Witt stayed with Snook and his many enterprises for ten years.

"We developed a wonderful working relationship," Snook says of her. "She did all of my correspondence, my books, my appointment setting. She was a most efficient secretary."

The secretarial help would allow Snook the extra time to create the Q.L. Snook Insurance and Real Estate Agency. He now had four thriving businesses: teaching, life insurance, construction and the agency.

These businesses became Snook's passion. He enjoyed every moment of his work. All seven days a week of it, working seventy-to-eighty-hour weeks. Q.L. kept this incredible pace for the next fifteen years. During that time he managed to save a good percentage of his earnings.

"Margaret and I set a goal to save twenty percent of everything we made," Snook says of those early years in Champaign. "We didn't have any problem with that, and really saved more than that."

Snook operated his businesses and organized his work week with great passion. His enthusiasm for his endeavors was unbounded and infectious. He truly loved what he was doing.

In time, however, he saw that more prospective customers were not in the construction side of the business, but in the insurance side, particularly in the life insurance area. It also was clear to him that insurance was a business in which he could make large commissions all year long, even in the non-construction winter months in Illinois.

Snook operated his construction company from 1946-1963. Nora Witt managed his office for the construction business as well as the insurance and real estate company.

With Snook's passion for selling insurance came his philosophy of service to the customer, value and spirit of commitment. It was simply too hard to say no to Q.L. Snook. He so believed what he represented, it was unthinkable that people would jeopardize their families and not buy from him. Often, he simply wouldn't leave the home of the prospective client until they said yes after Q.L. was able to answer ALL their questions!

Snook rose quickly in the Land of Lincoln Life Insurance organization, and through his innovation, he became vice president of the company. Snook soon built a network of agents throughout Illinois to represent the company as well. He personally trained and coached all of his agents, teaching them his unusually successful selling methods, infecting them with his spirit and enthusiasm and encouraging them with his unyielding confidence that "everyone needed their product!"

He treated his agents with respect and paid the highest commissions allowable. He flew them to conferences and training seminars, often conducting them himself. He had faith in winning, confident that he wouldn't, or couldn't, lose. His personality was inspiring for anyone who came into his employ or who had contact with him. Many of his agents would claim that "An aura of confidence enshrouded him."

Snook's efforts catapulted Land of Lincoln to great heights of success. In his final year with the company, Snook directed sales of $6,700,000 and obliterated the existing sales volume records of the company. He could have easily stayed with Land of Lincoln, but that wouldn't be his destiny. Fate would take him down another path.

Q.L. remembers that earlier in his life, however, jobs were scarce during the Depression and his parents worked long days for the benefit of their family. Clayton Snook accepted what jobs he could to feed his family. Q.L. recalls his father supplying vending machines in the area with candy and crackers. While always a temptation when he'd walk by the boxes of candy waiting to be distributed, he knew it was the family's livelihood and would have been wrong to take a candy bar anyway. In addition to stocking machines with the boxes of candy, the elder Snook fixed broken vending machines, and often had a supply of them near or even in the house in Bloomington.

From their house, church was about a four-mile hike for the Snook family. They attended the Second United Brethren Church. While the family had a car, they walked more often than not. Q.L. can remember that his dad was usually tinkering with the engine to keep it running.

After church, the pace of the walk home was more leisurely. While mother stayed home to cook for the seven children, the rest of the family would stop, pick wild flowers along the roadside, discuss the sermon and spend time with each other. During the summer, when driving, they would often stop to purchase a block of ice. Once home, Q.L.'s mother would make ice cream for a Sunday afternoon treat. The kids would vie for the ice cream dasher, a tasty treat that was always loaded with ice cream.

The two-room schoolhouse in those early years of Quentin's life was not far from their rural home. The teachers were a husband and wife team, Mr. and Mrs. Dewey Fristoe. The Snook children had a distinct advantage over the others because the Fristoes rented a room in the upstairs of the Snooks' two-story home. It was precious income and extra cash for the family.

Mrs. Snook also advertised tourist rooms to rent when they had several people stay a night or two as they traveled along the highway. During summers for young Quentin, the strangers that stayed in the house were always a fascination. Where had they come from? Where were they going? What stories had they to tell? For the Snooks' other renters, the school teachers, he had to be far less inquisitive, lest they give him an impromptu lesson!

Quentin's mother sometimes fed the guests and her family breakfast, lunch and dinner. While he didn't know it then, the income from these boarders and one-night lodgers was important income for his mother and father.

Because their home was also used as a roadway hotel, the Snooks took great care to keep the appearance of their home up, as well as the landscaping surrounding it. Quentin remembers the dedication his father and mother displayed in keeping the lawns, shrubs, garden, and flower beds well groomed. A row of tall maple trees stood between the road and the house. In all, the Snooks had about seven acres. A row of poplar trees stood on the opposite side of the house. Encircled with these tall maples and poplars, the home was shaded against the hot summer sun, and shielded somewhat from the cold blasts of Arctic air in the winter months.

In the front yard, Q.L. remembers an immense Colorado Blue Spruce. It was a perfectly shaped tree, a handsome landmark that could be seen from a long distance. Its conical shape was beautifully formed. In the winter, the spruce would gather the fresh fallen snows and hold them in delicate balance on its sturdy boughs. The children often played around these evergreen boughs, shaking them and laughing as the heavy snow would land on the woolen-wrapped back of a child. His father was once offered two hundred dollars for that Colorado Blue Spruce, but he turned it down.

Although the national news was chaotic and often depressing, Quentin's mother and father maintained harmony and peace in their family.

"I never heard my folks fight," Snook says of those growing up years. "My mother was a kind, but firm woman, always taking time to encourage us, clothe us and feed us. She was always inquiring about our school work! Dad often needed to work two jobs to keep us fed and sheltered and still managed to take the time to be with us children."

Snook recalls seeing them embrace frequently and speaking softly and quietly to each other. Conflict in the family was dealt with quickly and fairly, and rarely, as Q.L. recalls, with harsh or loud outcries. If there was conflict between his parents, it too was resolved without argument.

"If my dad grew very quiet and distant, we all knew not to bother him. I can remember dinners when we all sat and ate together during which time the kids would be chattering and clanging forks and knives together and my dad wouldn't say a word—quiet as a mouse in church. Don't know what was on his mind. He gave no clue and no one asked. Probably the strain of work and other problems, but none of the kids ever knew of it."

Neighboring families were also an important part of growing up. They had friends for miles around them. It was common practice that neighbors would barter with each other for goods and services. Clayton Snook would often help fix a screen door for Hanna Summerland, a widow who lived in Bloomington.

"It was a different time then," Snook says wistfully. "Everyone helped everyone else. You never thought about it, you just did it."

In school, Quentin had his best friends. He spent what time he could with them, balancing after school work for his dad, and time at his fruit and vegetable stand. There were Frank Robertson, Edwin Smiley, and Orville Mohr. He grew up with these guys, rode his bicycle with them, played baseball with them. They were friends throughout their elementary school years.

Snook remembers his childhood with fondness. Caring parents had busy lives in their efforts to support their family. Understanding parents listened to him, encouraged him, and gave him all the support they could. He remembers his father's unique listening philosophy with a smile and warmth in his eyes.

"My dad had a quiet demeanor. Never saw him get riled or angry. I would ask him for something, or ask his advice on something, and he would usually answer my question with a question! He'd let me think about the answer, maybe even ask me how I would answer myself! In the end, he taught me the value of common sense. He taught me to rely on my own answers and conclusions, and to be wary of taking other people's advice, even his!"

Q.L. can remember his father working for a local furniture company for a while, collecting past due bills. Times were difficult and people would often not be able to make payments on furniture they had purchased.

"My dad had a soft way of approaching these people, letting them know of their obligations, and how the furniture company needed to have their payments on time. He would sympathize with them, but always tell the other side of the story, after he listened to theirs. I'm sure he heard every excuse in the book!"

These lessons by example would be put to good use in later years by Q.L. He, too, learned to listen with understanding, yet remind clients of the importance of paying on their obligations in a timely manner. Snook credits his father for many, many habits in his life, of which this was one.

Work stability came to the Snook home when Q.L.'s father borrowed enough money to start a portable feed mill company. The portable mill was mounted on the flatbed Ford truck and would be driven from farm to farm and the feed mixed and ground according to the farmer's specifications and needs. Q.L. and his brothers were expected to help their father by opening and closing gates, enabling him to drive onto and away from the farmer's property. Ground feed was for the livestock. It was important that barn doors, gates to pens of animals, to pasture and the main gate on to the farm were quickly secured by me, my sisters and brothers when helping dad.

"We had feed for every kind of animal that existed in twenty square miles! Feed for cattle, chickens, horses, pigs, rabbits, you name it."

One incident that Q.L. will never forget, and that shaped his own philosophy, happened one day when his father went to rest his hand on the iron guard rail that covers the gears of the grinder. Accidently, his hand missed the rail and slipped into the gears, shaving off one finger and part of another.

"As a result of the accident, my dad needed some doctoring and couldn't work for awhile."

A family friend and distant relative, Hartwell Howard, came to see Q.L.'s father. Howard was a local builder and contractor in Champaign and was a wealthy man. He had taken a liking to Q.L. early on and came often for visits. On this particular visit, however, Q.L. remembers that Howard offered to loan his mother and father money to pay doctor bills and assist them in getting by until the elder Snook could go back to work.

Q.L. remembers the long discussion between his mother and father about the generous offer. Reluctantly, they agreed to borrow three hundred dollars from their benefactor and friend, Hartwell Howard.

"The day that Hartwell came to deliver the money," Snook recalls, "my dad changed his mind. I'll never forget what he said. He told Hartwell that three hundred dollars was a lot of money, and that if something were to happen so that he couldn't pay it back, it wasn't worth losing the friendship that they had between them. He couldn't take the money. They would get through this time some other way. Well, Hartwell rubbed his bald head and replied, 'I've made a lot of loans in my life, but I've never been turned down after I've offered before!' "

The lesson learned from that day stayed with Q.L. Snook all of his life. It is not advisable to loan money between family or close friends. If anything were to happen and that money couldn't be repaid, the relationship might be damaged, or worse.

Q.L. states, "No matter what you are borrowing for, never borrow from family or friends. Borrow from a bank, or borrow from an investor. Make a loan from a bank, but not from a family member or close friend. Friendship is far more important."

The Snooks survived that accident and went on to replace the portable mill with a permanent five-story mill. It was state-of-the-art technology then, according to Snook. At the mill, farmers could store their grain, getting sacks and truckloads of feed for any type of animal, and keep running accounts. The Snook Feed Mill became a larger and larger business, and one that

Q.L. was active in from his childhood until well after his father's death in 1955. The mill claimed his father's life.

"My only daughter, Sarah, was born on Saturday, April 16, 1955," Snook recalls. "I was so proud to have a daughter, after three sons, that I drove the fifty miles to Bloomington from Champaign to tell my dad the news. He was elated. We hugged and he shook my hand, happy and proud to have another grand-daughter."

The next day, Sunday, the elder Snook went to church and then to check on things at the mill. When he didn't return, Q.L. got a call from his mother, telling him that his dad had accidentally fallen in the mill.

It was Q.L.'s brother Wilbur, who had found his dad at the mill. His father had died from a fall that later was thought to be from the top, on the fifth story of the mill.

"I think he must have taken the elevator up to the top to check on some things. His glasses were found there, five stories up. He probably wasn't feeling well and took his glasses off to wipe his brow. We think he had a heart attack and, as he struggled to get to the elevator door, slipped and fell from the landing."

Snook had lost his beloved friend and father the day after his daughter was born.

After his father died in 1955, Q.L.'s mother asked him to manage the feed mill operation. His older brother Wilbur had been at the mill with his father for all of Wilbur's life. Genevieve knew Q.L.'s eye for business, and she wanted things in order at the mill. It was a time of strain in the family, as is often the case. But Snook did what he could to take charge. The mill was fifty miles from his Champaign office and Snook either flew or drove the distance as often as necessary for over four years. Later, the mill was sold in 1961 and Snook's mother moved to Portland, Oregon, to live near Snook's youngest brother, Herbert.

Clayton Snook was by far the most important influence in Q.L. Snook's life. He says that "he loved his father," and missed him terribly. He attributes many of his successful business practices to his father, and learned how to care for his family from his dad as well.

"The role of a father is to care for his children. Nothing complicated, but often with much sacrifice and hard work," says Snook today. "I just don't understand anyone who doesn't fulfill that obligation. If you father children, they are your responsibility until the day you die, or they die."

Snook wistfully admits, however, that he didn't inherit or adopt all of his father's characteristics, and he is the first to confess that he doesn't have the patience that his father had, or the unique ability to listen to his children as much as his father did. He recalls his father as his best friend, always willing to listen, even if he didn't solve young Snook's problems. Even as a grown man, Q.L. had an unusually close relationship with his father.

"My dad was always interested in how I was doing, how I cared for my family, how my business was growing. He was concerned when I borrowed money to buy my first house on Ells Avenue in Champaign. Although I knew what I was doing, he still cautioned me on going into debt."

Clayton Snook also believed in his son Quentin.

"He told me that he knew I'd be a success in business some day," Q.L. says softly. "My business was just beginning to grow when he died, and he never saw anything of what was to come, of course. For me, well, I had no idea what success was yet."

A motive for profit

Q.L. learned early in life that there isn't such a thing as *a sure bet* as it relates to money. That might go without saying, but when you're a kid and the bank closes, *with your money in it*, the lesson is tough to learn. But learn he did. *Even after you've earned and saved your money, you can still lose it!* It wouldn't happen again. He had been broke once, even though he was just a kid who lost money in a savings account at the Liberty State Bank during the Depression, but it wouldn't happen to him again!

Snook adopted the business philosophy and it ran deep into his personal life that he rarely did anything unless he had a chance to profit. If he saw the opportunity for profit and service, he would often direct intense energy, endless hours of effort and work and a *never say die* attitude toward achieving his goal.

Comments

What a privilege it is to write about Q.L. Snook. My husband and I first met Quentin when he was a student at the University of Illinois, and he lived part of that time in our home. This was before his marriage to his wonderful wife, Margaret. Through those fifty-plus years we highly prized their friendship. They're a good team! We witnessed their steady progress through the years. As busy and involved as Quentin's building, business and community service projects kept him, his care for family and humanity ran strong. He cares for God and for his family and friends. He reaches out to people and recently helped me in my time of need after my husband passed on. My husband and I were only two of the many, many people he and Margaret have touched by their kindness and friendship.

Lois T. Meyer, Belleview, Washington

Mr. Snook combines the elements of a successful man. He has been successful in business and given back to his community many times over through civic and political action. I wish him every success.

Jeb Bush, Candidate for Governor of Florida, Coral Gables, Florida

I first met Quentin in the fall of 1946. We were both students at the University of Illinois. I was in agriculture and Quentin was in law. Housing was hard to obtain in Champaign, and after looking long and hard I heard it might be worthwhile to contact Quentin. He had built a

75

house in Champaign for himself and Margaret. I talked him into building an apartment in the basement to rent out, but when he said he couldn't afford the materials, I gave him $75 for the first month's rent to use to buy the needed material. We lived there for two years and moved upstairs after Q.L. built another home and moved. We still keep in touch through an exchange of Christmas cards. Following his career in the newspapers, he has done very well for himself. I'm proud to have known him.

Dick Carlisle, Retired Professor,
University of Illinois, Carterville, Illinois

I have known Mr. Snook for thirty years and I have been inspired by his determination to do all things well. He has prospered in business. He has also been most generous in giving financially to the churches he has attended and the organizations he supports. I do admire him.

Dr. Ralph Nast, Champaign, Illinois

Quentin L. Snook has had a very interesting and fruitful life. I met him in the Champaign-Urbana Kiwanis Club. He was an active member and dedicated to serving the people of his community. I remember his interest in promoting the Boy Scout organization over a long period of time. The Scouts could rely upon him for support of their various enterprises. He did not limit himself to the support of any single organization, but was a supporter of any worthwhile project that served his community.

Harold W. Scott, Professor Emeritus, Urbana, Il.

3 FORMING SUCCESSFUL RELATIONSHIPS

Margaret Snook and the importance of a good marriage

Quentin Snook was a shy kid growing up. He studied hard in school and occupied his time after school working for his dad. He had little time, or interest, in the social skills, such as dating girls. Q.L. smiles when he says it, but he was actually afraid of girls!

Deep down, Q.L. wanted to meet someone he could marry.

Q.L.'s sister Ruth Marion suggested to him that he should meet a friend of hers. He reluctantly agreed to meet her and a blind date was arranged by the two girls, who were classmates at ISNU.

Margaret McArthy lived in Illinois State University Home Management house on Normal's campus. She was shy and nervous about the date as well. Margaret wasn't very outgoing, but was pleasant and willing to meet him. She wasn't sure what kind of a match she and this young man might make.

"I went up the steps of the house and knocked on the door. When it opened there she was," Snook says, laughing. "I introduced myself and was taken with her right away. She smiled and said, 'Well, come right on in!' And so I did. I felt like she was inviting me into *her life*, rather than into the house!"

The couple talked about trivial things, and agreed to see each other again. They didn't know it then, but both were instantly interested in each other. Q.L. liked the fact that she had been raised on a farm. His father had told him that "The best girls to marry are ones from the farm." Snook reasoned that it made sense, but really never doubted the logic. Farm people were hard workers as a rule, with good character and a helping way about them. Margaret seemed all of that to him.

In a short time, Q.L. and Margaret became well acquainted and in 1946 they were married. During their engagement, Q.L. began construction on his first home in Champaign. He needed a home.

Like his parents, Q.L. found renters to help defray the cost of their newly constructed house. Snook taught college courses at Illinois Commercial College and built more houses, specializing in time with the Sears-constructed *Stylecraft Home* line. Margaret, meanwhile, also taught school that first year of their marriage. In subsequent years she would be a substitute teacher, and would eventually teach in more than thirty-five schools.

Like her husband, Margaret Snook was conservative. She, too, had been a saver, and a thrifty person. She helped Q.L. when and how she could during those early years, mainly in the area of offering good advice.

"Q.L. would come home with a problem and we'd talk about it, trying to find the right solution."

Soon the couple had their first child, Quentin, Jr. While Q.L. was busy with his construction company, selling life insurance, and his teaching, Margaret tended to the baby. A second son, Maurice, would follow, and then another boy, Tom. It was in 1955 that the couple had a baby girl, Sarah. Their fifth child, Earl, was born two years later.

As busy as Q.L. was with building his business, he never neglected his children. On flying trips, his kids often accompanied him. On weekends, the family always tried to do something together. As the children grew and got into their own activities, it was often Margaret and Q.L. that volunteered to be leaders in various organizations that involved their children. Whether it was 4-H, scouting, church, or school activities, the Snooks believed that they needed to be there. Keeping up with our busy family was fun for all of us being together.

Despite a priority on involvement in the activities of one's children, running a successful business places great demands on one's time. As Q.L. Snook reflects on his life, he wishes that he could have "listened" more to his children. He remembers the way he was raised, with his father always having an attentive ear for him, yet Q.L. acknowledges that he often "vetoed ideas" that his children had before they had a chance to fully express them.

"I wished I would have listened to my kids more as they grew up," Q.L. reflects. "I never neglected them. They never lacked anything, but I would encourage parents to stop for a moment, listen to their ideas, their activities and their thoughts. Like my father did when I was young, he was there for me, not just as a provider, but as a listener as well."

What time that Snook couldn't give to his children, Margaret made up for, however. As a devoted mother who was active in their daily lives, she knew that her husband was busy at making a good living for them. It was a part of their upbringing. Women raised their families, and men provided for them. Q.L. and Margaret had that understanding early in their marriage and it has worked well for them.

Typical of Q.L.'s life then, and today, he is on a rigid time schedule. It is an obsession with him that he readily admits. He cannot waste time, not even a moment. That philosophy was truer in his earlier business years than perhaps today, but to know Q.L. Snook, you have to *know his schedule,* and be able to fit into it.

Satisfied clients can open
doors to prospects

In the life insurance industry few have equaled the successes of Q.L. Snook. He learned the business quickly, studying the methods of some of the best agents in the field. His philosophy was that everyone needed life insurance, and that no excuse was a valid one for not buying, especially from him.

With Kansas City Life, Q.L. drove himself hard, working long hours, scheduling every minute of every day, trying hard not to waste any precious time. He had found the vehicle to make him wealthy, and no one was going to slow him down.

During his association with Kansas City Life, Snook developed a selling method that no one at the time, at least to his knowledge, was employing. This selling technique was one that he perfected, and it worked extremely well.

"Most insurance salesmen wait for referrals from the company to make their calls. I didn't have time to wait; I needed to find my own referrals."

So Snook developed a referral system based upon the clients he had. In time, he had his clients "pre-selling" for him, and had all the referrals, and sales, he could handle. The referral system created by Snook was revolutionary in the company at that time. It later became common practice in professional selling and is still used heavily today. Snook used it to advance his selling career, significantly increase his income and, subsequently, set sales records in the company. He would use the referral system for the rest of his selling, management and company building career.

The system was fairly easy, on the surface. It starts with belief in yourself, and belief in your product. Snook strongly believed that every family needs adequate insurance. He shared that enthusiasm with his prospective clients, driving home the point that we have obligations for our family's welfare and financial security, living or deceased. His argument made sense to everyone that heard it. First, he created desire.

"Once people see the sense of it, you need to create an immediacy, a strong desire to purchase the protection, immediately."

Money was often the issue between closing and not closing a sale. Q.L. learned from his father years ago that the best way to answer a question, was with a question. By having the client answer their own objection, the business of selling becomes easier, less driven by the salesman, but still directed. No matter what objection was offered, Snook would listen carefully, rephrase the objection and ask the client to answer it.

The process works like this:

Question: "I just don't think we can afford the premium."

Answer: "Can you afford not to have the benefits? I understand your concern. Your money is tight. If you can't afford this premium, how much can you afford?"

By answering the question with a question, the client is then forced to think about what they can truly afford. Few people would admit that they can afford nothing. According to Snook, that isn't in our nature. So, an answer usually comes. An amount usually is offered. Through this selling method, learned from his father's treatment of his own questions, Snook would explain that they truly could not afford to live another day without a life insurance policy. How much was enough? He simply showed them how long the family could meet the cost of living if the client died tomorrow. His enthusiasm was a powerful persuader.

"If you can afford a policy of $25,000 of life insurance and your family currently needs $25,000 a year to live, eat, pay the mortgage and debt, then your family would be able to survive one year after your death, assuming there were no funeral costs."

The argument made sense. Who wanted to leave their family destitute, being able to survive one year, or two, following their death?

Snook believed it himself. He wasn't selling anything he didn't believe in, and it was evidenced by the amount of insurance he had on his own life. He had a wife and children, and they also would need to survive if he were to die tomorrow.

"Often," he would argue, "it isn't a matter of how much you can afford, how can your survivors afford the cost of living should you, their provider, die tomorrow?"

Once the sale was made and Snook was convinced that the client saw the common sense and reasoning behind this protection, he was also sure that he could impart his unique referral system to get new clients that he could *share the important news with.* It worked like this:

As he completed the sale, Snook would go over it carefully, and congratulate the client on making a wise and judicious decision. Telling the client that he wished to share this information with others, could they provide him with a name or two of someone they were close to that he could call on? There would be no obligation! No hard selling! Just a chance to praise the client for making a wise decision about the future of his family!

With each name the client would offer, Snook would *qualify them.* Questions such as: *Is your brother working? How large is his family? Do you think he has insurance already? What is his approximate age?* Specific questions were asked to pre-screen the prospects and give Snook clear direction as to which he should concentrate on first. He called his method, *More Mileage From the Referral System,* and gave several seminars and presentations about his successful system of finding sales prospects. His presentation to agents and groups alike would go as follows:

All great things have their beginnings. The referral system is no exception. It was created out of a necessity to satisfy the creative desires of man to inform his neighbor about an event which would serve as a mutual benefit.

This system is as old as man himself. Its use faded somewhat by the innovation of modern advertising.

Great progress was made through paid media of advertising with a national cost amounting to billions of dollars a year in the United States. This high cost, together with the difficulty of being able to measure an accurate incidence, has brought the idea of the referral system back into use. However, its importance and results have received more attention of late because of the refinements. This brings us to a step-by-step process whereby the aggressive salesperson of today can realize unlimited dollar sales volume with considerably less effort.

It is not my intent to shorten the sales process. We, as sales-minded people realize that the four basic stages in the sales process must be met: attention, interest, desire, and action. Furthermore, let me remind you that it is assumed that you have skillfully covered every item thoroughly with the prospect in the sales presentation. This is an opportunity to invest in the best and most modern, up-to-date combination life insurance investment program available today. More people can be reached with group meetings by qualified referrals.

Now that the sale appears to be complete—this is where the elite salesperson of today starts developing an unlimited list of qualified referrals that are presently being denied an opportunity to qualify for the Universal Life plan. It should be pointed out right here that it is assumed that <u>everyone desires</u> and <u>wants</u> to participate in this program. You begin by asking this question, "Mr. and Mrs. Jones, of all the things I have said this evening, what one *thing causes you to believe that this is the wisest investment decision that you have ever made in your lifetime?"*

Wait until the customer answers that question. Profits for shareholders comes through sales activity. Yes, that's right.

As our sales progress, there is the possibility of more interest from those who can qualify. The more sales that are placed, the fewer advertising costs are involved, which means more value available for distribution because people like you are carrying the message to others. Now this is where YOU come into the picture. We have discovered that over ninety percent of our sales have come from people like you, Mr. & Mrs. Jones— people of good reputation here in this community.

You are liked and looked up to. We need your help in making this opportunity available to more people. Wouldn't you like to help? Naturally, I wouldn't be here this evening had it not been for George Smith, your good friend, who has qualified for this plan. Therefore, I am asking for some people that you think could qualify for the Universal Life plan with tax- deferred cash accumulation. You probably could think of dozens of people, but I could only see three to five people that you think would listen to me and be excellent boosters like yourselves—and can afford to save money.

In order to get the five names, use the reminder in this order: F.B.S.—Family, Business, Social, repeating after each name an inquiry as to their willingness to Listen - Boost - Afford to Save Money. These names are placed upon the last sheet of the necessary information sheet to be left with the prospect. This list should be names of people you don't know. When it is complete, go over the list, bringing out the thought that you don't know these people. Say: "I wonder if it would be better if you would contact these people first? It might be comfortable for them since they don't know who I am."

After completing the list of names in this fashion, congratulate the client on being able to qualify just as George Smith (the referred party) qualified. You have given him a farewell by a handshake. Then, just as you begin to leave, you suddenly stop, saying: "Say, today is Tuesday, could you have seen all five of these people by Friday?" Give a three- to four-day lead time. Upon receiving a firm commitment, ask for an appropriate time to call on Friday. 6:30 p.m. is usually a good time, or would 9:00 a.m. Saturday be better? Be sure that you follow up and call at the exact time on Friday.

When you call, congratulate the client on giving you those five names. Then inquire about the first name on the list. How did this individual respond when you talked with them? Repeat this on down the list, making notes of their comments.

When you are certain that each name had been contacted, then you proceed to call these referred names to make your appointment. "Hello, Mr. John Doe. This is Bob Long of Golden Rule Insurance Company. Did Mr. Jones tell you about an unusual investment opportunity? Fine. He asked me to take thirty minutes to show it to you. Would Tuesday at 7:05 p.m. or Wednesday at 9:10 p.m.

be suitable? Fine. Do you and your wife work together as a team? Good. I'll be there at 9:10 p.m. Wednesday at your home. I'll mark it on my schedule. Will you mark it on your calendar? Fine. I'll see you Wednesday at 9:10 p.m."

Any phone questions such as, "I don't have any money," or "Tell me about it, over the phone," should be answered by saying, "Mr. Jones, George Smith asked the same question. After I finished showing it to him, he said that it wasn't like anything he had seen before. That's why he asked me to show it to you. George asked me to take thirty minutes of your time. Would 7:15 Tuesday or 9:10 Wednesday be better?" Repeat this after each and every question until you get a favorable answer.

You are now on your way to becoming an elite sales person with a built-in system of a perpetual inventory of names of real people waiting to see you. Why should they be left out? Why should the customer be permitted to deny his friends an unusual investment opportunity? Do you believe in his investment one hundred percent? Do you have the courage to deny someone an opportunity to invest if he fails to believe one hundred percent by failing to let his friends in on an excellent opportunity?

This referral system, as given, will work. It is guaranteed to work. It will average two to three new customers when used properly. Try it! People will say, "Joe knows where the money grows!"

To the client you give a list of the five names. The form does not have to be elaborate, but make sure you

90

jot the names down, and give it to them. It may look something like this:

You Can Help Your Investment Grow

Yes, we need your help and in helping us *you will be helping yourself* as many others are doing. The more people who know about this investment opportunity, the faster it will grow and the more it will be worth. How can you help? By simply giving us the names of five qualified people like yourself, that can afford to save money and invest wisely. These may be friends, relatives, business associates, fellow club members, neighbors, etc.

The necessary information sheet will be in triplicate for:

Copy 1: client
Copy 2: company record
Copy 3: agent record

Name_____

Name_____

Name_____

Name_____

Name_____

*****

The agent's form will look a little different, but will be equally as important.

Name_____

Address_____

City_____State_____Zip_____

Phone_____Age_____
Employment_____
Marital status_____
Social Activities_____
_____

Your list will be the same as the client's list.
1.Name:_____
  Service rendered_____
  _____Date_____
2.Name:_____
  Service rendered_____
  _____Date_____
3.Name:_____
  Service rendered_____
  _____Date_____
4.Name:_____
  Service rendered_____
  _____Date_____
5.Name:_____
  Service rendered_____
  _____Date_____

    While the plan is simplistic, it is highly effective. Without ever calling on the new prospect, Snook made calls back to the client he had just sold to receive information as to when the client had talked with the referral. When the client had called the five referrals extending an invitation to see the plan, Snook noted any response the client heard from the new prospects.

They would become *his qualifiers, his salespeople!* If they did show interest, Snook would make the call, set the appointment and go in to make the sale, already pre-qualified!

Snook perfected the five-name referral system. The system worked only when good records were maintained, proper follow up was executed and a positive, enthusiastic approach was being made. He became proficient at the skill of appointment setting by always giving the client two choices: Monday or Tuesday? One p.m. or two p.m.? He always had an answer ready, every possible objection was answerable, usually by asking a question back. He became doggedly persistent, yet never lost that wonder of enthusiasm and the belief that *everyone needed adequate insurance!*

Soon Snook had all the prospects he could handle. He knew from experience how many he could close out of the five names. He knew when to back away and when to charge ahead. He became proficient at his craft, and sales were pouring in.

Q.L. Snook began selling life insurance at the age of twenty-five. During that first year he set a goal for himself. He set about a schedule to work seven days a week, seventy hours a week, using his referral system.

Relationships in the military

It would seem that the statement, *apply your talents where they fit,* would be a natural thing to do. It would made good sense. For Q.L. Snook, it also made good sense. He is fond of this principle of success by using the following statements:

"Work at a job you love, and it isn't work at all."

"If it doesn't fit, walk away from it."

"Enjoy what you do, and you won't have enough time to do it."

Snook has learned this principle the same way many people do, the *hard way.*

Snook wanted to go into business, but the thought of financial reward told him that perhaps law school would be the faster way to financial independence. He embarked on two of the most frustrating years of his life.

"I worked two jobs and still went to law school at the University of Illinois," Snook says of those times. "I worked hard, really hard, but the studies just weren't coming. I really wanted to go into business, but I hung on, and hung on. I should have started my business and worked at something I really enjoyed, rather than thinking I'd make a good lawyer."

It was a hard lesson. The man was obsessed with time, having just spent two years at the University of Illinois, graduating with a bachelor degree after completing student teaching at University High School and at Urbana High School in Urbana, Illinois.

But those classes in law school were not wasted. With complicated business deals ahead of him, proxy fights, formations of companies, stock sales, the experiences of law school would stay with Q.L., even though he regretted the loss of time.

"I'm surprised that most people really hate their jobs," Snook marvels. He can't imagine not doing what he wants to do, even though the work is hard and long.

When he enlisted in the navy after the bombing of Pearl Harbor, Snook meant to be a pilot. He had his private flying license. Snook was sent to Lambert Field to become a navy pilot. He was serving his country and doing his part.

While at Lambert, Snook volunteered to teach flight operation, and he was given the job of teaching several classes. This was something that piqued Q.L.'s interest. He had always loved to teach, to offer assistance and to help others.

After a year in the navy, Snook's painful back condition, caused by years of lifting feed sacks at the mill, was worsening. The pain was with him constantly. A "convenience discharge" was given to him. Upset and determined to make up the lost time, Snook returned to Bloomington and immediately picked up where he left off, helping his father. With the military behind him, he could resume his life, his hopes and aspirations. But another surprise was waiting for him.

He received a draft notice to be inducted in the army! The army was looking for soldiers to fight the war in Europe and Snook was the right age. Never mind he had just been discharged from the navy; the army wanted him now!

He was drafted into the army and there he would languish through basic training, infantry training and, finally, heavy artillery training. Once again, Snook found himself in uniform, and waiting to be shipped overseas. The only relief from his chronic back pain was to lie totally supine on the floor, totally still. Then he would get a few uninterrupted hours of sleep before work would begin the next morning.

As orders for duty in Korea drew near, Snook underwent a complete physical. Upon evaluation, an army physician was surprised that Snook was even in the army. "How did you get in here?" he asked. "You have no business being in the army. You have third degree spondylitis and really need surgery. I'm recommending discharge and a forty percent disability."

Floored by the doctor's report, Snook couldn't believe his ears! Discharge! Disabled! Surgery! None of this fit into his schedule of things! Once again, he took the discharge. He wanted nothing to do with the disability. He had no time for a disability!

Another year of his life was spent pursuing something he didn't want to. He grew more and more obsessed with making up for the lost time. The harder he worked and drove himself, the more convinced he was, it wasn't fast enough to make up for all the lost time. He was determined to become successful. He just needed time to do it!

Although he had little to do with the events that brought him into two branches of the military, Snook was determined that he would never again pursue something he knew he shouldn't do. From his army discharge on, Snook would focus on his plan, his schedule. Little or nothing would ever take him away again from his plans, his hopes and his dreams. Nothing, that is, for many years. But years later, Snook would find himself fighting for his business life.

He would listen to the words of advice his father gave him, "If it doesn't fit, walk away from it." And he would walk away from it.

Maintain an honest relationship
with the Creator

Religion has always been a part of Q.L.'s life. Ever since he was young, his mother would rouse everyone from Sunday morning slumber and they would head on down the road, walking to church. She would stay in the house, however, and prepare a meal. Church has always had special meaning for Q.L. It is God's house. It is a place where one can go to listen, learn, pray and be with others of the same faith.

But a person's relationship with the Creator, according to Snook, has little to do with church attendance, and even less to do with the facade that some people maintain who "put on a church face, but live some other way."

Q.L. grew up attending the United Brethren church in Bloomington, Illinois. The teaching of the time was fundamental: belief in Christ as Savior, belief in the Bible as the Word of God, and a strong emphasis on living with an honest and reverent heart. The United Brethren later merged with the Methodists and the church became the United Methodist Church. Both churches sprang from the Reformation period in history, adopting similar ecclesiastical structures. The United Brethren Church was founded by William Otterbein, who had strong ties with the Methodist movement and its founders, John and Charles Wesley, in the mid-1700s.

The church values that Snook learned in those early years became part of his essence and rarely did he question their validity. More than anything, Snook believes that a person must *live the Christian experience*. In business, of all places, Snook believed in utmost honesty and practices above reproach. Not everyone shared that philosophy, as Snook was to find out later, but for him it was more than a matter of good living habits; it made the profound into common sense.

"Every lie, every dishonesty will come back to you," Snook says. "We pay far more for the misrepresentation than we can ever imagine, far more than we could ever gain from it."

This simple philosophy Snook has lived with his entire life. There is right and there is wrong. If you don't know the difference, go to church and find out.

In his youth, Q.L. was also introduced to the Christian Science Church. The intellectual bent of the church's philosophy spoke to Snook, making more sense than the many "acts of faith" needed to believe in certain Bible stories. Snook became fascinated with the writings of founder Mary Baker Eddy, particularly her book *Science and Health with Key to the Scriptures*, first published in 1875.

Within those writings, Eddy taught that the body and mind were intimately related. What the mind thought and focused on, the body responded in kind. If we fed the mind positive, healthful thoughts, the body would respond with good health and vitality. Conversely, doubts, negativity, fear, uncertainty and painful thoughts that our mind became occupied with would be manifested within the body as disease, unhealthfulness, pain and suffering.

Mary Baker Eddy's writings professed that if our body was in pain or disease, that we needed first to change the thoughts and activities of our mind; and if we did, the pain would subside, or disappear completely.

As Snook grew and the years of lifting feed sacks for his father took a toll on his back, he looked for relief from his pain, and found some hope in the writings of Christian Science. Driven by a strong desire for accomplishment, it made sense to Snook that if he adopted the philosophy that mind rules the matter of the body, perhaps it would offer relief from the chronic pain in his lower back.

As is always the case with Q.L. Snook, he displayed zeal and fervor in this new faith and belief. There was no allowance for mere interest; it was all, or nothing.

Following painful separations in the navy and army, which were both humiliating and time wasting in his life, Snook sought counsel with the wisdom of Mary Baker Eddy and Christian Science. He did so quietly, without fanfare, as is his way. In the months that followed his *re-programming* through Christian Science, Snook is convinced that a "scientific healing" took place. The chronic pain in his lower back began to subside, and although still present at times, he was able to focus on work, not on pain. He continued the

Christian Science practice and believes to this day that he had a "religious healing." Not miraculous on an evening of revival, but gradual, through diligent practice, and supplication. While chiropractic physicians could bring him some relief, he wasn't going to have back surgery. With treatments from physicians in medical science, and belief through religious science, his pain subsided and, gradually, all but disappeared.

Snook probably would have continued in his fervor for Christian Science, but as so often the case, people have a way of getting in the way of us and the Creator.

"I was young and just starting out in business and couldn't afford to pay regular dues to the church," Snook says of the pressures he felt from the local church group. "I couldn't afford to give in those early days. I just didn't see a correlation with my faith and belief in Christian Science and the constant need for money and gifts."

Because he couldn't give with regularity, the local church dropped him from the roll. He was incensed.

"It really turned me off. I was living testimony of the power within the philosophy of the church, but was treated like a second-class citizen because I couldn't afford to take precious dollars that my family needed to live on and give them to the church."

The event would keep Snook away from organized religion for fifteen years. As his family grew, Snook poured his time and attention into business, not church. He had been dealt a painful blow, not by God, he reasoned, but by small-minded people.

In business Snook embodied the teachings of his youth and the experiences he had with Christian Science. The fundamentals of good Christian living were lived everyday by Snook in his business dealings. He never wavered from them.

"I've been tested so many times," he says. "So many times I could have done something under the table, cheated the company, cheated an employee. No, sir. I never did and never would. That would be the worst thing I could ever do."

Snook's fundamental belief in the Bible and its teachings for living, as well as his belief in *feeding the mind* with positive thoughts and healthful attitudes, have combined within him to make an interesting blend of philosophies not found in one discipline or church. But it has worked for him.

"My dad always said to me that a clean mind is a clean body. How can I maintain a clean mind with unclean thoughts? It just doesn't make any sense to live any other way!"

As Snook's family of five children began to grow, it was his wife who saw the need for them to be schooled in matters of religion. Going back to his roots, the Snooks decided to enroll them in the Methodist Church in Savoy, Illinois, a suburb of Champaign. Although he felt good about his children's religious training, he hadn't resolved his own feelings about church, the people and our relationship to the Creator.

"One day, the superintendent of the Sunday school that my kids attended asked me if I'd teach a high school class. I guess he knew I'd been a teacher and knew my kids attended, so he thought I might say yes."

Snook told him that he didn't feel qualified to teach the Bible. And with his unique brand of personal faith, wasn't sure he would even want him to teach. He assured him it didn't matter, but Q.L. pressed the matter further.

"Suppose I taught the kids two stories of creation," Snook argued. "Would it make a difference? What about the Apocrypha, which includes additional books of the Bible? Could that be taught in your church?"

He was told it was all right. Methodists were "open-minded" and would welcome his thoughts.

With that said, Snook agreed to teach. He didn't join the church, but agreed to teach. Once committed, Snook took on the project with fervor and enthusiasm, spending hours preparing lesson plans and encouraging his high school kids to question, think, ponder and study, so that they might find the truth as they saw it, not necessarily the way some minister or church leader might see it.

The class grew. He encouraged them to seek the truth on their own, to live the teachings of the Bible, and to live the life that God would have us live, not just talk about it.

With his ability to arouse interest and stimulate ideas, Snook exhibited his enthusiastic belief that *everything and anything is possible.* "Program your mind for success and it can be yours!"

Even before all the great literature about positive thinking was written, Snook was living it and teaching it. Had he been a writer, he could have authored those books as he lived the philosophy of positive thinking with passion and conviction.

The Sunday school class became well attended . Not surprising, Snook was approached by members of the administrative board of the church to help solve others problems as they related to church school attendance.

"Why are some classes needing teachers?" Snook asked. He cites that the church was certainly large enough. Usually only about one-third full on Sunday mornings, many of the classrooms were dark and silent following the service.

He was told that they couldn't find teachers to administer the classes. Snook wouldn't accept that explanation. When asked if he could help recruit, Q.L. took the project on with his usual enthusiasm and confidence. If they found the kids to attend, he'd find the teachers.

"I approached people in that church, and some outside of the church as I was, saying that there was a great need to fill. They had to meet my criteria and qualifications, which mainly involved the desire to help, but I never recruit for anything without screening the candidates."

Meeting criteria? Qualifications? Snook approached some of the most capable people in the church. He demonstrated the need, and asked them point blank to serve that need.

"Everyone needs to be needed," Snook says of human nature. "It doesn't matter the setting, everyone wants to feel like they are important and can make a difference. Well, almost everyone."

Using his own unique approach to people, Snook recruited from within, telling people of the great need and the great importance of the job. Soon every position was filled. The church was busy ordering books and teaching materials and the place was buzzing with energy, new life, and new hope, all because people were asked. Classes began to fill up because there were teachers eager to teach.

Snook later served as superintendent and continued to teach his own class for several more years.

"You can fill any need, win at any good cause," Snook says, "If you have a plan, and recruit those around you to help with that plan. People don't want to do things for the rest of their lives, but everyone can jump in and get the thing started."

Not only did the church have a full slate of teachers, but Snook made sure that every teacher had a backup, who went in training to become next year's teacher, as well.

Over the years with Methodist churches in Savoy, Illinois, and Deltona, Florida, Q.L. has also been asked to raise money for church projects. People quickly realized that he had an ability to do this. Snook believes that it is only a matter of selling the need and the purpose.

"Believe it or not, the church in Savoy didn't have an indoor bathroom!" Snook couldn't understand it. His house was plumbed, as were most homes. Why wasn't God's house? He took the challenge upon himself. The church needed plumbing.

"In business, the way to raise money for any project is to get a plan, and take the shortest and most direct way possible to achieving your goal."

Snook asked the minister if he could have a few minutes of time during the Sunday morning service. Graciously, the pastor agreed. Snook stood up and proceeded to point out the obvious, this was God's house, and God's house deserved to have an indoor bathroom. He had done his homework, and knew how much the work would cost. Now, pacing back and forth on the altar, in front of the Sunday morning worshipers, Snook proceeded to raise money the only way he knew how, to ask for it.

"It will only take $2,000 for this project," he began. "My wife and I will donate $100 each." Snook pressed his captive and slightly uncomfortable audience. "Who will raise their hand to pledge the $1,800?"

Silence. Deafening silence filled the sanctuary! He waited. The silence grew louder. Still he waited. Finally, he had to break the ice.

"Well, we really wouldn't want it that way anyway. Everyone should have an opportunity to get involved. Will anyone pledge $500?" He waited for a hand. Still no response. "How many would be willing to give $100?" He waited. And he waited. Finally a hand went up, then another, and another. In all, eight people pledged on that Sunday morning. The seed money for the bathroom was in place.

On another occasion the superintendent told the congregation that a new minister had been appointed to the church. But upon inspection of the parsonage, we all saw that it couldn't be used. The former minister hadn't told anyone about the water in the basement. Again Snook addressed the congregation in his direct manner about raising $10,000 to buy a parsonage and still not add to the existing mortgage payment.

He implored the congregation, urging them to give. He announced that he and Margaret would donate the first $1,000. Who would join them? Again the faces fell and no one responded. Again he asked. Surely they couldn't let their new minister live in a house with water flooding the basement with each rain. Surely! Finally, one woman raised her hand and gave $1,000. Then another gave, and another. Snook's passionate message was heard. "Sell the need and the purpose, and you will find your results."

Although uncomfortable to some, his methods were effective.

To Q.L., religion doesn't have to be named Methodist or Baptist, Catholic or Jewish. It is a way of life, a code of virtue and honor, which everyone *should live* if they profess to be a believer. Snook wears the same face in church as he does in business, as he does in his own home. It is his way; it is his faith.

Although Snook has been a contributor to churches in Illinois and in Deltona, Florida, he now insists upon being asked for his help to teach, raise money, or to become an active part of the church business. He has led capital building drives, donated housing for local ministers, even given property to the church on several occasions. But he involves himself with a certain amount of caution, and now lives by the notion that he must be asked and then given the latitude to accomplish the goal in the manner which he deems best.

Simply put, that is Q.L. Snook.

Comments

I have known Q.L. Snook the last nine years, and in three different roles, you might say. First, he was a mentor to me when I opened my practice here in Champaign nine years ago. He freely gave of his business knowledge and savvy, which I respect. Some time later I knew him as a patient. Later I knew him as a friend. Once he stopped by my office for a visit and invited me to stay at one of his

properties in Florida for a family vacation. I took him up on it, and we had a special Christmas vacation to Disney and other places. The trip wouldn't have happened but for Q.L.'s good heart. That's just the kind of person he is.
Dr. Peter J. O'Brien, Champaign, Ill.

I've known Q.L. Snook for many years. He has been, and continues to be, an inspiration to me. I believe it was in 1956 when I interviewed him as a part of a college course I was taking. The interview was fascinating and very educational. I specifically remember his mentioning the three C's involved in borrowing from a bank. He explained that a banker considers character, capacity and capital capabilities of a borrower. We've remained good friends over the years, and I continued to ask him for advice as I built up my simulation business. It was extremely helpful. "Q.L." had a hand in numerous businesses but was always "one of the guys" and very down to earth. "Q.L." always had time for civic activities which included the continual development of the local YMCA.
Rudy Frasca, President, Frasca International, Urbana, Illinois

4 MAKING A COMMITMENT TO SUCCEED

New heights in life insurance

Of all Q.L. Snook's entrepreneurial ventures, success in life insurance became his crowning achievement. A natural salesman, Snook struck gold in his early years selling insurance and paved the way for his future success and for many others in years to follow.

He got into life insurance accidently. As a teacher at Illinois Commercial College Snook had already mapped out his future. He loved teaching and although the pay wasn't good, it was providing an adequate living, combined with his contracting business in Champaign. But the story has already been told when, and how, Snook would leave both professions behind to become one of the most accomplished men in the life insurance business.

"When Margaret brought that insurance salesman through the house to see me I was hoeing weeds in the backyard garden. I didn't have time to see any salesman! I was on a schedule!"

But that salesman and his company, Kansas City Life Insurance, would alter Snook's future and would lead him in a direction he never could have imagined.

"When he told me I could make up to fifty percent commission on sales, I dropped that hoe in the dirt, grabbed his arm and said, 'Come on in, we have to talk!'"

Snook spent several years with Kansas City Life. He received his insurance license, was thoroughly trained and ready to sell policies. That's all Snook had ever wanted—independence and control of his own future.

He found business where people never looked. He so thoroughly convinced his customers of the great importance of life insurance that they willingly gave him leads of family members, friends and acquaintances to call on as well. Snook never needed the company's leads like other agents; he generated plenty of qualified leads on his own, with the help of his satisfied customers.

"I couldn't get to all the leads that were generated from this referral system," Snook says, laughing. I ran from early in the morning until late at night, seven days a week."

The sales volume that Snook generated was staggering. His persuasive, yet genuine, salesmanship was not easily rejected by customers. He had an answer for every objection.

"Life insurance is something everyone *has to own*," Snook advises, even today. "It naturally appealed to a person's desire to be responsible and care for their family."

In 1958, Snook heard of a new insurance company being formed in Illinois. He was intrigued and attended one of the company's formation meetings where stock in the new company was being sold. Founders Art Thomas and Ray Powell were raising capital and needed investors and hard-charging sales agents and agencies to sell for them. Snook listened to their plan and decided to join them.

Land of Lincoln Life Insurance Company opened new doors for Q.L. Snook just as he opened many doors for Land of Lincoln. In its formative months, Snook not only invested in the new company, but was appointed the company's vice president. He not only sold the insurance offered by Land of Lincoln, but began to travel the state of Illinois conducting shareholder meetings.

Snook hired a secretary, Nora Witt, in his Champaign office. She handled the tremendous volume of paperwork created by her boss, sometimes three and four sales in a day's time. Additionally, Nora handled the intricacies and daily activity of Snook's construction company, all the subcontractors that were involved in several building projects, closings, financial matters, and, of course, the new sales that Snook generated in his spare time.

Within three years, Land of Lincoln Life had become a large Illinois company, thanks mainly to the efforts of vice president Q.L. Snook.

Snook's efforts with Land of Lincoln weren't going unrecognized by the competition, either. A much larger and better capitalized company soon came knocking on his door. Republic Investors Life Insurance Company could offer things that Land of Lincoln simply couldn't: more money, a more aggressive management, and a much larger geographic area in which to organize and sell. The Arkansas company was licensed in many states, while Land of Lincoln was licensed only in Illinois. The offer they made Snook was too good to pass up.

Snook sold his stock in Land of Lincoln for a profit at the time. In his three years with the company, the stock had gone up in value. Snook had even held stock sale meetings for the company and had personally sold many in attendance. Republic Investors gave him several attractive options, including a large block of ownership of stock and the title regional director for the company.

But the bubble would burst at Republic Investors. Snook began to see signs within the ownership of the company that bothered him. He was so focused on selling insurance that rarely did he direct his attention to internal matters. Why should he? The company was growing and sales records were being set. What internal problem could interfere with this success?

When the company began to offer stock splits and promote them as two-for-one, or four-for-one splits, Snook began to see what was happening. He began his own quiet investigation and soon realized that all the evidence he could gather suggested that the company was committing acts of fraud that began to alarm him. The company was making plenty of money in new sales, but seemed to be getting greedy and the periodic stock splits smacked of impropriety, something that Snook couldn't tolerate or be a part of.

Snook had personally sold many of the Republic Investor stockholders and now feared for them. He himself was a large stockholder. Therefore, he decided to take a bold step to protect the stockholders who had invested in the company. If the company were ever found guilty of fraud, they would be shut down, their license to sell insurance revoked and every stockholder, regardless of the size of his investment, would lose.

Snook became acquainted with a Chicago lawyer, Richard Peterson, representing an association of stockholders against the company in a proxy fight. Their goal was to get one member of the association on the board. The proxy fight became important when Snook uncovered damaging documents that supported his belief that the company was indeed making loans on questionable real estate in another state.

The proxy fight lasted over a year. Snook invested a large amount of money into it, as did other key stockholders. In the end, they won the right to put one person on the board of Republic Investors.

The proxy fight at Republic Investors took its toll on Snook and aversely affected his ability to sell its insurance enthusiastically. In the end, three former officers of Republic Investors Life Insurance Co. of East Moline were indicted by a federal grand jury on fraud charges. The indictment involved transactions in connection with the sale of their own company stock to the public during the years 1961 and 1962. Stock had been sold to insiders at a rate of one to two dollars per share and then resold to the public at between four and ten dollars per share.

The *Champaign Courier* reported in 1964 that *"The spotlight was turned on Republic Investors Life after a bitter proxy fight led by Champaign businessman Q.L. Snook. The charges brought by Snook against the three men resulted in a $7.7 million libel suit against Snook, John Ennis of Urbana and others. The libel suit was dismissed in August 1964, with prejudice against the plaintiffs and without cost to the defendants. Snook said, 'I had sold stock in Republic Investors to a lot of people and I intended to protect their interest.'"*

With the lawsuit and proxy fight behind him, Snook devised and began to set in motion a plan to create the largest capitalized life insurance company in America. He wouldn't be a part of someone else's dream again. This time, he would create his own company, build his own business empire, be the innovator of his own organization, and take it to the top of the entire industry. However, providence would take him in another direction. The stakes were enormous and the risk was equally large.

The Q.L. Snook Securities Company

In March of 1963, after years of working in the insurance and construction business, Snook decided to expand into securities and formed the Q.L. Snook Securities Company. The experience of buying and selling securities for his clients would become invaluable to Snook.

The business plan that Snook promoted to open his securities company in early 1963 cited that the company would supply a need for those who were looking for an opportunity to invest money in an industry that could experience tremendous growth. All of Snook's studies and research pointed to the life insurance industry as the best place to put his clients' money.

Snook's securities philosophy was different from many other companies of the day. He believed that it was the small investor whom his company should serve, not the large one. Few securities companies were serving this growing market, and Snook soon learned to serve it well.

He developed a logical, step-by-step approach whereby the small investor would have a greater opportunity to accumulate wealth. His plan started with regular savings. He encouraged his small clients to save regularly from every paycheck, no matter what the amount. The savings plan that Snook drew up for his clients varied, but the philosophy of the plan never varied. Before any other bills are paid, pay yourself.

Save ten, fifteen or twenty percent, if you can, but regularly take money and put it away.

Snook knew that any investment plan needed to have immediate appeal or the desire to continue with him might wane. His counseling was solid, however, teaching patience and some sacrifice so their future would be secure. He was telling his clients that the future need not be feared. Any fear can be diminished, however, if one is willing to use some of his present income in a systematic plan *now*. His logic made sense and his counseling was appreciated.

The securities company was organized with a select group of twenty-five investors, who believed in his goal and served as a "vanguard" in helping him carry the word to others. Money was invested in minimums of $1,000 each from his core twenty-five. In return, he gave them a certificate of ownership. In order to demonstrate his faith in the project and encourage his "vanguard of investors," Snook wisely agreed to underwrite the original issue with no commission charge to the corporation. Additionally, he agreed to absorb all the overhead expenses of the company for the first year of its operation. With this innovative start, how could an investor lose?

Snook received the state charter for the company in February of 1963 and a dealer's license followed shortly after. By June of the same year Snook posted *profits* of $40,000 on an original investment of $132,000! Thirty percent profit in six months! This type of gain was almost unheard of in any securities company, much less a new one. With no overhead costs, Snook returned a handsome dividend for his investors right from the opening bell. The six month profit/loss statement of his company didn't take into account the numerous small clients of the company who had purchased stock in life insurance companies that would, he hoped, some day realize excellent gains on their investments.

The balance sheet for Q.L. Snook Securities Company of December 31, 1963 showed assets of $200,000. Retained earnings for the company were $178,000 and net earnings at $17,500. Gross profits exceeded $40,000. By year's end, 1964, assets of the securities company had grown to $240,000, with retained earnings of $220,000 and a gross profit of $50,000. Net earnings for Champaign Securities Company, renamed in 1964 from Q.L. Snook Securities Company, were $36,000. Snook paid dividends to his investors from the first year of his company.

Snook's clients were almost always small investors. He had become a champion for the average Illinois resident, always taking the time for careful explanation, minimizing risk for his clients when he could, and standing behind his investment strategies with his own money. Snook wouldn't consider doing business any other way. It had to be above-board and honest. If he couldn't invest in a company after careful analysis, he never sold it to anyone else. His primary investment companies were Land of Lincoln Life, which he represented already and knew very well; Republic Investors Life, Great American Corporation, Franklin Life Insurance Company and a handful of other life insurance firms.

An event would happen in 1963, however, that would change Snook's conservative philosophy of investing in only insurance companies. He would join a company called General Development Corporation. The corporation was made up of three brothers named Mackle. The Mackle brothers were developers and builders of entire communities, not just subdivisions. They were astute businessmen, "rising stars" of the construction industry throughout the state of Florida. The Mackles would eventually leave the General Development Corporation to create the Deltona Corporation. When Snook heard of their plans to build a Florida city called Deltona, an amalgamation of the names of nearby cities DeLand and Daytona, he just had to be a part of it. As one might expect of Q.L. Snook, when he put his mind to something, it usually was accomplished. So it was with an explosive idea to sell home sites in central Florida in a community known as Deltona.

General Development Corporation and the Mackle Brothers

In January of 1950, family friend and financier, Hartwell Howard, invited Q.L. and Margaret to his winter residence in Winter Park. He wanted them to drive him to Miami to see apartments that he had built there in 1920. Snook had no schedule or money for such a trip, however Howard had been a dear friend of the family and somewhat of a mentor for Q.L. Out of loyalty to his friend Hartwell, Snook made the trip to Florida out of Q.L.'s heart with respect to Hartwell, and, during that trip, he first heard of the incredible saga of the Mackle brothers and the General Development Corporation.

Hartwell Howard told Snook of the many developments throughout Florida that the Mackles were building. Whole cities were being designed and built.

Frank Mackle, Sr. was a talented German immigrant who built a fortune in real estate. He built entire communities along the East Coast with housing. When the sons of Frank Mackle, Sr. became old enough, he brought them into the business. But it was the strength of the three sons combined that would eventually make the corporation one of the largest builders in America.

Elliott Mackle was the oldest and had studied engineering. After his father's death in 1941, Elliott took over the construction end of the business. People who knew him say that Elliott Mackle was a wizard for spotting good development land. He presided over several Mackle projects including the entire construction of the naval base at Key West, one of the Mackle's prize developments. Elliott directed the company and developed communities such as Key Biscayne, Marco Island, Deltona, Spring Hill, Marion Oaks, and Opalocka, as well as naval installations in New Brunswick and Key West.

Robert Mackle was quiet and studious and excelled in financial matters. He worked the complicated financial deals needed to build the many projects of the Mackles. Robert handled the funding, borrowing, investor strategies and all of the financial records for the corporation.

Frank Mackle, Jr. was the salesman of the family. He also had excellent organizational skills and served as president of the Deltona Corporation. Frank oversaw the company's overall operations, which stretched from one end of Florida to the other.

Snook had seen the Key Biscayne project when he became acquainted with the Mackles in the 1950s. Hartwell Howard knew Elliott Mackle and his brothers and told Snook that the "Mackles were the best builders in the country." As a young builder himself, in Champaign, Q.L. knew that someday, somehow, he would be a part of the Mackle empire. His opportunity would come a few years later in 1962.

"I just had to be a part of that empire," Snook says with an almost reverent voice. "The Mackles were the developers of Florida, premier home and community builders. I knew they needed me, and I knew that Illinois farmers would love the sunshine."

Snook wrote the company and expressed his interest in becoming a dealer for them in Illinois. Neil Bahr, vice-chairman of sales for the Mackles, responded to his letter, saying that they already had a dealer in Urbana and that a dealership in Champaign would be a conflict of interest.

Not easily daunted, Snook went to the dealership in Urbana to work for them! His enthusiasm and desire to be recognized by the Mackles resulted in the sale of more property in three weeks than the entire agency had sold in three months! It also led to lots of commissions. That got the attention of Neil Bahr and the Mackle brothers.

Snook made another trip to Florida to try to convince them to give him his own dealership, but again, his efforts failed. No amount of convincing would bring Snook a coveted agreement to sell for the General Development Corporation. He was told that a conflict of territory would occur if they gave Snook an agreement to represent their efforts in Champaign. They wouldn't budge.

Although disappointed, Snook vowed that someday, somehow, he would represent the giant builders in Illinois. He knew he could outsell anyone the Mackles had. He would be their star salesman. They needed him.

His opportunity would come six years later in 1962. The Mackles had started development in Deltona. The Deltona Corporation was an immense project and needed tremendous organization to sell the several thousand acres of land to develop. The Mackles remembered the energetic Snook from Champaign, and this time they contacted him to see if he was still interested in representing them.

Q.L. Snook became the seventh franchised dealer in America for the Deltona Corporation. They gave Snook thirty-five Illinois counties to sell in, and sell he did!

Snook made several trips to Florida in his six passenger Cessna to view the 15,000 acres that the Deltona Corporation had acquired. Choice Florida property, "The land of promise!" It was a land so rich in beauty and diversity that Snook immediately fell in love with it. A lush green countryside blessed by the warm Florida sun and fresh breezes off the shores of the most magnificent lake that he had ever seen, Lake Monroe, and the dark and mysterious St. Johns River. The property had over twenty lakes and a systematically designed development plan that appealed to Snook's love of organization and planning. He was one hundred percent sold!

The Mackle development philosophy was truly unique. Instead of plowing up the landscape and building row houses, as did most the developers in the fifties and sixties, the Mackles were one of the first major developers in the country to build their communities around the landscape. They spared wooded areas, turning them into parks and nature preserves. They also built communities planned with zoning for schools, churches, business centers, parks, and golf courses. Mackle roads curved and wound around pristine lakes and through wooded home site areas. The township plat concept of square city blocks and perfectly symmetrical towns wasn't part of the Mackle scheme. Few city streets were straight. Many of them meandered throughout the community, dodging stately live oaks and magnolias, rather than bulldozing them. Mackle properties were known for their pristine beauty and harmony with the natural environment. They were decades ahead of their time in the building industry.

When Snook saw the "promised land" of Deltona and realized the enormity of the project, he became obsessed with it. Nothing could hold him back from being a part of the Mackle empire. Ever since he had heard Hartwell Howard praise them, Snook had wanted to be a part of their organization.

He created a plan to sell Deltona lots that was truly unique. Having convinced the Mackle brothers, he reasoned the toughest part of the transaction was over. If he could sell record amounts of life insurance, securities and homes in Champaign, Illinois, wait until his clients could see the paradise in Florida!

And, that's what Snook did. He brought his clients to see it personally. Hundreds of them.

Sales director for the Deltona Corporation, Neil Bahr, said this of Snook's efforts in Deltona.

"Q.L. Snook became a vital leader of our sales efforts. His enthusiasm for the Deltona community and boundless energy couldn't be easily turned down."

In typical Snook style, he sat down and developed a plan to sell the Deltona properties that would be extremely hard to refuse. His step-by-step plan, personal money-back guarantee, and service to his clients were unequaled at the time, even to the Mackles.

Through his vast network of clients from construction, real estate, insurance and securities, Snook had only to interest people in "taking a look at Deltona." He knew that once they saw what he had seen in Florida, that the property would sell itself.

Snook had a full-proof sales plan.

First, he sold his clients on the idea that buying a lot in Florida now would be the ideal and most secure investment they could make in their future. The climate and sun in Florida would replace the cold, harsh winters of Illinois. Few people needed much more convincing than that. Using his unique referral system, Snook soon had plenty of prospects.

Next, Snook would take his prospective buyers and fly them to Florida in his private airplane. Few people had ever even been on an airplane before, much less a personally escorted flight on a private plane to Florida. Snook had every detail planned. He treated his passengers like royalty, providing better service than the commercial carriers! Every flight was narrated by the pilot himself. Snook was first, and always, a teacher. He would point out rivers and cities, building excitement for their eventual destination. When they crossed the state border into Florida, Snook would often lead them in a song or toast upon their arrival. By the time his clients arrived, they were pretty much sold!

But Snook went even further. Deltona lots were selling for $1,000 in the beginning. He guaranteed every passenger that if the pristine beauty and features of Deltona that he raved about weren't to their liking, they were under no obligation to buy and any deposits would be immediately refunded.

Snook reasoned that few could turn down such an offer. He charged $50 for the flight, but wouldn't have needed to charge anything at all. "I charged only because people need to make a commitment."

The fees rarely covered even the expense of aviation fuel for the trip, but Snook didn't care. His commission for selling lots in Deltona would more than compensate him for the flight expenses.

Snook landed his party in DeLand at a former military airport. There he had his own car parked, waiting for the party. They would walk the few steps from plane to car and almost without a break, the guided and narrated tour continued. The drive from DeLand to Deltona was only a few miles, but Snook took them on a leisurely drive through the countryside, past deep blue lakes, through pristine wooded areas. His clients would see the "best of Florida" on the short, but well-planned, tour he had designed.

Once in the Deltona community Snook showed them the entire layout, carefully driving them down the freshly paved roads of the development. His guests saw model homes in appealing tropical colors such as green and pink. They were a welcome sight compared to the more conservative Illinois home colors.

Snook had been one of the first to purchase a lot for himself. He let everyone know that not only had he bought a lot, he had a Mackle-built home on his lot. His guests would be taken there and often spent the night before the flight home. A good meal and fellowship were part of the relaxed plan. The next day his clients would see their "retirement" lot they had previously purchased.

In all, Q.L. Snook and his network of agents in Illinois sold 1,000 lots in Deltona. Limited to five lots for each investor, Snook often sold five at a time, citing the "investment opportunity of a lifetime!"

It wasn't sales hype either for Snook. He believed in Deltona and its future. He became a major investor in the community and still owns many properties in Deltona, including a home where he and Margaret reside.

Not only was Snook's presentation of Deltona unique, so was his selling method in Illinois. The Mackles' sales plan created by Neil Bahr called for distributors and agents to advertise Deltona, selling the warm Florida sun and advancing the idea of a long, enjoyable retirement. But Snook found a better way, a way that, once again, was unique to him. He became so successful in selling Deltona lots that Bahr and the Mackle sales team invited Snook to Miami, to their headquarters, so that he might teach the entire Mackle organization his sales method. Never one to reject a teaching assignment, Snook enthusiastically agreed to go.

He had tried the Mackle sales approach of paid newspaper advertisements, but found the medium expensive and without much energy. It was hard for the newspaper ad to really expound on the virtues and natural beauty of Deltona. So he brought the beauty of Deltona back to Illinois with him, and began selling property in Deltona.

Using his camera, Snook brought back pictures of Deltona and Florida. His presentation was practiced and perfected and taught personally to every agent who sold Deltona for him. Snook and his unique presentation style not only created energy and enthusiasm, but also desire. He wanted his prospective client "to be able to taste Deltona." In usual conservative fashion, Snook also sold the retirement and investment advantages of Deltona to his client.

Nothing about the Snook presentation of Deltona was unrehearsed. He had a sequential and systematic approach to presenting Deltona that few could resist. Every possible objection would be anticipated and an answer prepared. If the beauty of Florida couldn't sell them, then the investment plan of owning a piece of the Sunshine State might. If that wouldn't convince them, then the cold and bitter winds of January in Illinois and their future retirement plans might. He never missed a beat, selling just enough, never wasting more time or energy than he needed to.

But where did his prospective client list come from? Snook had an answer for that, one so effective that the Mackle team adopted it throughout their company, selling the Snook referral system throughout the nation and to overseas investors. Snook had used the referral system before and would use it again.

The Snook referral system starts with one prospect. It may be a friend, a family member, a former client, a fellow Kiwanian, a member of the same church, a neighbor or a business associate. Snook maintains that if you find the first prospect you will find hundreds more. In fact, he guarantees it.

When Snook made his rehearsed presentation to the prospect, one of two things would happen: either they would buy from him, or they would not. But in either case, Snook reasoned that they would know at least five people. If they bought from him, he was sure that they would want their friends and neighbors to know about the fantastic opportunity in Florida. So, he would ask them to consider giving him some names of people with whom to share the news. Eventually, the conversation would lead to five names. Five was the magic number for Snook's system. With five qualified referrals, he was assured of selling two or three of them.

Following the sales presentation and signing of the necessary information sheet, Snook would then lead his client into the referral names. Once given the five names of close relationship to his new client, Snook knew that it would still be a cold call for him to contact them. Even with the name of his client, he would not know the referred names, nor would they know his. So, Snook would ask his client, or prospective client, to talk to them for him!

"Can you see Tom by Wednesday at 5 p.m., or at 7 p.m.?" Snook would ask. The client would think of their relationship with Tom and answer yes or no. "Wait for an answer," Snook counsels. When the desired answer comes, confirming that the client will telephone or talk to prospect number one, move on to the next prospect, prospect number two. "Always get a day when they will have been able to talk with the new prospect."

Snook says that the beauty of this referral system is that the client is doing all the prospecting. With the client's name in hand, the door is usually wide open. "Any salesman worth their salt should be able to walk away with a contract."

Follow up is the key to successful referral selling, Snook advises. Before you leave the client's house, you should have five prospects, five names and their relationship with the client, and days and times of the day that they will have contacted them.

The next step is not to see the prospect, as might have been guessed. Snook calls the client back and confirms that *they indeed have seen the prospect, or talked with them.* A lot of information can be gained from the client. How did they respond to the idea? Were they receptive? Would they like to see someone who can explain it further and answer questions?

With five prospects and five confirmed contacts with those prospects, make the call. The prospects have been qualified and confirmed. The toughest part of the sale has been made. With those five prospective sales, the odds are in your favor that with a well-rehearsed and objection-free presentation, the sales person should be able to close two or three of them, possibly all five. Then the process repeats itself, getting five more prospective clients' names from each of those sold clients.

"In time," Snook says, "you will be hard pressed to see all the qualified prospects that you have found."

Using this five-name referral system and a well-orchestrated plan to get all the needed information from them, Snook has built company after company. He uses the system even today, as do sales organizations throughout the world.

"We only have twenty-four hours a day. Use every second productively." For Snook, the philosophy hasn't changed in his seventy-four years. His schedule simply won't allow it.

Q.L. Snook was honored by the Mackle brothers time and time again. "His brand of service and commitment was unequaled," says Neil Bahr, Deltona Corporation sales director.

Snook believed in his product. He believed in Florida's growth pattern. He believed with all his heart that every person who could afford it should purchase a lot in Deltona. What sold for $1,000 in the early 1960s has increased in value fifteen to twenty-five times.

Today Deltona is a city of 58,000 people, the second largest in Volusia County, and it is still enjoying rapid growth. Deltona has recently passed an election to become a city, and has highly-qualified city officials, such as current mayor John Masiarczyk and his city council. Over 25,000 homes have been built in Deltona since the first paved roads were put in by the Mackle brothers. Snook had contractors build several houses in Deltona, and they still are increasing in value. He became his own best client, and today, all of his clients who bought from Snook and his associates in the 1960s thank him as well. Many call it the "best investment they have ever made."

The Snook referral system helped catapult Deltona sales. Over 1,000 lots were sold by Snook and his network over the next few years. He sold them either for cash, or as little as $15 per month. He gave service to his clients and prospective clients that got the attention of the three Mackle brothers.

Snook had sold lots at Marco Island, Spring Hill and Sunny Hills, Florida.

Snook was not only an important sales agent for the Mackles in Deltona, but they used him for training as well. As a keynote speaker in the 1964 Annual Deltona Corporation Sales Convention, Neil Bahr, vice president of sales for Mackle, sent Snook this letter of thanks:

Just a note to express to you my personal appreciation for the valued contribution you made to the success of our just-concluded 1964 Convention. As usual, you were in fine form and your message was "solid," to say the least. As I expected, I heard many fine comments concerning you and your presentation and would like to reiterate our pride in having you as an integral part of our team. Once again, my sincere thanks and best wishes.

The Mackle brothers final project was the development of Marco Island. A place of spectacular natural beauty to lure visitors and home buyers, Marco Island became the focus of an international battleground between Mackle Development and environmentalists who were determined to leave the pristine white sand beaches of Marco Island alone. In the end, Audubon and other environmental concerns forced the Mackle bulldozers to shut down. Projects that had been granted approval by federal, state and local officials were disapproved, and the Mackles were blocked from further development. Instead of filing bankruptcy, the Mackles refunded millions of dollars to investors, banks, and clients who had purchased lots only to find out that they couldn't build.

While the Mackle fortunes were vast, the Marco Island "last paradise" brought them to near financial ruin. In *The Last Paradise* by Douglas Waitley, the author concludes that:

"All could have come true for the Mackles in Marco Island but for the denial of two vital dredge and fill permits that were blocked by political groups under pressure from environmental concerns. Frank Mackle believed that the Corps (Army Corps of Engineers) didn't play fair with him.

"Yet oddly, these very denials, with the precedent they set, made Marco Island unique. Never again would such a waterfront development of finger canals be allowed. Marco became, in effect, one of America's last such paradises.

"In the end, Frank Mackle walked away without fanfare. As he left his office for the last time, he was overheard quoting a famous general, 'Old soldiers never die, they just fade away.' "

Little did Q.L. Snook know when he helped sell out lots in Deltona that he and the Mackle brothers had more in common than he ever realized. He would know the success of hard work and intricate planning, but, like Frank Mackle, he too would mutter, "Old soldiers never die, they just fade away." He too would one day hand over the keys to a large company that he had built, in a hostile bid for power and control after a bitter fight to save his creation. Like the Mackles, he too would know the bitter disappointment and deep sting of failure brought on by other men's greed and personal interests.

Manage your future

His years with Kansas City Life, Land of Lincoln and Republic Investors had taught Snook a great deal. He had done well with all three companies and had become a leader in the field, an innovator of new products, new ideas and a top-flight motivator.

As the proxy fight with Republic Investors was drawing to a close, Snook began to formulate another innovation. In his mind he played out the scenario. He studied the progress of the good companies and observed the traits of the unsuccessful or stagnant companies. He articulated his goals:

1. Make more money for his stockholders than they were now making.

2. Give the customer a better product with more benefits than they were getting.

3. Give more opportunity to his employees and agents than they were receiving.

It was Henry Ford who lived by the business philosophy that "it was not good business unless the buyer and the seller benefit." Snook believed that.

Snook knew that there were two basic ways of starting a company. The first was a small, sole proprietorship or family-held company which began small, grew slowly, but where the owner(s) retained control of their future. The second was to start big, gather investors, sell stock, raise the needed capital and open as a major industry player.

As the idea of forming a life insurance company grew in Snook's mind, he called a friend of his who was also sales director for Republic Investors, Bill Sharp. The two met over dinner and Snook opened up to him, telling Sharp of his plan. Snook had already made up his mind. He would set out to create the largest initially capitalized life insurance company in America.

The two men talked throughout the evening and then well into the early morning. As they talked, an even more ambitious plan began to take shape. Why create only a life insurance company? Why not capitalize sufficiently to create a large conglomerate, perhaps the largest holder of companies in America? The idea excited Snook. If anyone could do it, he could!

The idea was to create a shell company, a holding company and fund it adequately so that the companies they purchased or began were already major players in the industry. Insurance was to be only a part of it. They could purchase a bank, other insurance companies, residential and commercial income-producing properties, and innovative companies in other segments of American business. All of these businesses would fall under the umbrella of the holding company.

The two men imagined creating an American icon! But they weren't idle dreamers. That wasn't Q.L. Snook's idea of capitalism or empire building. If he could envision it, he could build it. If he could see it, he could construct it. He would build the largest initially capitalized life insurance company in America. Needed were three vital ingredients: character, capacity and capital, the three "C's" that Snook had built a small fortune on already. Unlike Republic Investors, his management would have the utmost character and honesty. Snook wouldn't have it any other way. The company employees would need to be above reproach and morally sound. He would need to hand-pick his organizational team and his board carefully.

The capacity of his company would be limitless. The holding company idea that Snook advanced was revolutionary in the early 1960s. The American conglomerate wouldn't emerge on the scene until a decade or two later. The design was simple: a small, well-chosen board of directors would oversee the operations of the holding company. They would be the visionaries. They would investigate other companies to purchase, looking for every opportunity to advance Snook's simple formula for success:

1) offer an excellent return on investor dollars;

2) offer more benefits and a better product to the consumer;

3) offer a better place to work than similar companies, so as to attract the best talent available.

The holding company would then appoint separate directors of each company started or purchased. On that board would be at least one of the holding company's directors. Their job would be to manage the company, hire the employees and ensure the profitability and smooth operation of the company.

Snook called a meeting at his brother's home in Bloomington to discuss the idea with his handpicked men that he would need to form the company and implement his ideas. They had many issues to overcome such as licensing the new insurance company that Snook wished to start, putting together a funding plan, creating a business plan, organizing a sales force. Could he interest anyone in this grand idea?

The answer was immediately obvious. Everyone whom Snook invited came. They were the best of the best, men who had been a part of Snook's business endeavors.

Don Cheatum was a man Snook had met at the Dale Carnegie Institute. A compassionate and highly capable sales leader and motivator, Cheatum had taken the Dale Carnegie Institute and expanded its influence throughout America. If Snook could recruit Cheatum, it would be his job to organize the effort to sell the stock, and then set up the organization to sell the insurance for the new insurance company. Cheatum was a high-powered executive, and although a friend, Snook had no idea whether he could land him. Would Cheatum give up all that he had accomplished with the Dale Carnegie Institute?

Snook knew that he would have to be persistent to successfully recruit Don Cheatum. Q.L. had not forgotten the story he'd learned in high school about Christopher Columbus. Turned down eighteen times for a ship to explore the open seas in search of new lands, Columbus asked Queen Isabella of Spain the nineteenth time. That one was the successful try. Then faced with insurrection from his crew and old myths and legends about the flat earth, Columbus set sail, failing to find the East Indies, but discovering a new world in the process. The story inspired Snook. It meant that a person must try and try and try again if they are to succeed. They must never give up. All that is needed is a good plan, in addition to faith and determination to succeed.

Could he form the largest initially capitalized life insurance company in America? He could. Like Columbus, he simply wouldn't take no for an answer. He simply wouldn't quit until he had realized his dream. He knew he could do it.

Snook's organization team included a longtime personal friend, Rodger Bliss. An independent agent, Bliss had the rare combination of honesty, work ethic and loyalty that Snook sought. He was a wizard of a salesman and had built a large agency. Later, Snook would sell his own insurance agency to Bliss.

The main men in place, Snook laid out his intricately-detailed business plan. The stock sale was limited by law to one year. If all of the stock was not sold in that time, every investor would need to be completely reimbursed. The non-negotiable time frame was therefore set for them.

The next phase was to raise $4,000,000 with which to capitalize the insurance company, Thomas Jefferson Life Insurance Company of America. With plans set, each man knew his individual task. They all agreed to go forward. Snook had personally recruited each man. His first hurdle was out of the way. Snook knew that he had some great obstacles to overcome, but he also felt there wasn't one that he couldn't surmount. Not even the well-prepared and detail-oriented Snook, however, could anticipate all the obstacles that would loom in the next few years.

Snook's goal with Thomas Jefferson Life was to build the largest life insurance company ever to be formed in the United States. The initial stock offering to the public would be four million dollars.

His plan had several phases. The first was to start a holding corporation. He would build the holding corporation with twenty-one pre-incorporators, each investing $25,000. Each of the pre-incorporators would have the right to purchase an equal amount of shares of stock in the life insurance company. The stock was to be issued at a value of two dollars per share.

The issue price of the life insurance company stock was five dollars per share. Once proceeds from the two million share offering were raised for the holding corporation, Snook planned to sell another 800,000 shares of stock that would be offered to the public to purchase into the life insurance company. Snook planned to sell these shares to 15,000 stockholders in Illinois, and had a detailed plan of how that was to be accomplished. He would use his unique referral system and train agents to use it properly.

Once the capital was raised, Snook reasoned that his company not only could sell life insurance competing with the largest companies in the state, but also purchase small companies licensed to do business in other states, allowing for rapid expansion.

It was a grand plan that Snook fashioned. No company in America had ever been formed with such a large number of shareholders. Few companies would have ever been formed with such a large cash reserve, either. Through acquisition of other companies, Snook wouldn't have to wait for the process of licensing his life insurance company in other states; he would simply acquire other licensed firms and, eventually, he would grow his life insurance company into one of the largest in the United States.

Snook took his time to set up the plan. He had spent two years planning this company and had written a detailed, step-by-step business plan which, when implemented, would enable him to succeed.

His first task was to find the pre-incorporators who would lay the foundation of the holding corporation. Again, he took his time. His selection process was deliberate. Not only was he looking for them to invest $25,000 each, with the risk of losing it all, but to be active and participate in the operation of the company as well. He wanted them scattered throughout the state, allowing for their sphere of influence to be large enough to attract the investors that the second phase of the formation of the company would call for. Snook's reasoning for this can be summarized in a simple phrase that his dad often shared with him:

"A farmer never plants his seeds in one place."

On November 15, 1964, Snook successfully brought twenty-one pre-incorporators together at the Holiday Inn in Champaign. Pledging their support of money and influence to sell the public offering of the stock, the company was formed. The twenty-one pre-incorporators pledged $600,000 in cash. The seed money was now in place. At the meeting Snook announced:

"Tonight we go from private offering to a public offering of common stock in the holding corporation. We are on our way!"

At the November meeting Snook laid out his plans to raise the other $3,400,000 needed in common stock in the holding corporation, so that his goal of $4,000,000 could be reached. He set a limit of 500 shares per person at two dollars per share. With a limit of $1,000 per person, his plan was to find 3,400 stockholders to purchase the remaining available common stock of the holding corporation.

Snook also detailed his next phase of the business plan. Once the $4,000,000 was raised, they would receive a permit from the state to begin selling stock in the Thomas Jefferson Life Insurance Company. That stock would be sold first to shareholders of the holding corporation, and secondly, to the public, a total of 15,000 investors throughout the state.

The life insurance sales goal that Snook set was $100,000,000 in the company's first year: aggressive to say the least. Snook's plan was that the life insurance company would make a profit in its very first year! This

145

was an ambitious undertaking that left even his ardent supporters scratching their heads. Could he really accomplish all of this? If he could achieve what he proposed, Snook's company would be one of the first companies in American business history to make a profit before they went into business!

The stock plan was so large, it would be the largest offering on record for a life insurance company in the state of Illinois in terms of the number of shareholders. Snook wanted lots of stock and he wanted everyone in the insurance business, including agents, to have the opportunity to purchase stock. Once they owned a piece of the company, they would sell it, encourage their friends to buy it, and advance the goals of the company that much faster.

The twenty-one pre-incorporators who formed the nucleus of the organization were: John Ennis, Kenneth McGrath, Ernest Smith, J.M. Spector, Harry Kinzinger, John Howarth, Llewellyn Rieke, Charles Grimes, Raymond Bane, James Scanlon, Kenneth Imig, Harry Holloway, Edwin Aylward, Lester Berry Smith, Richard Peterson, Q.L. Snook, Donald Cheatum, Ray Peters, R. Wessels, R. Janko, and Claude King.

Plans for the new life insurance company were often published in the local papers. Snook had chosen Champaign, Illinois, as the home of the holding corporation and the life insurance company and let the town know about it. Gathering support from throughout the community, Snook presented his plan to area businesses and civic groups. All of Champaign could benefit from such a large company headquartered there. Snook carried the message that seventy percent of Illinois life insurance buyers presently bought their life insurance from out-of-state companies.

Snook's second phase was no less ambitious than his organizational phase that included mobilizing twenty-one pre-incorporators. Now he planned to sell $3,400,000 in stock in the holding corporation to individuals at two dollars per share. The company would have one year to accomplish this sale, by Illinois state law.

All monies earned from the sale were to be placed in interest-bearing treasury notes and a full refund made if all the stock was not sold. Snook had thought it all through.

Now Snook needed a sales force to sell the stock within twelve months, an undertaking that even the bravest of security investment firms probably wouldn't attempt. Snook knew that, and that's why he would sell the offering himself, with hand-picked agents.

Snook had appointed Don Cheatum of Tolono to head his sales force. Cheatum and Snook reasoned that they would need 300 agents selling the stock for a full year to accomplish their goals. Cheatum was a qualified trainer. As a consultant with the Dale Carnegie Institute, he had been training salespeople for years in a highly motivating and challenging manner. Snook knew it would take the best of the best to select and train the agents that would implement the sale of all the stock.

Snook directed every phase of the plan. He was a major pre-incorporation stockholder, having invested $50,000 in the initial offerings. For control purposes, Snook wisely also purchased all of the "B" stock of the company, over two million shares. The "B" shares were for control only and did not share in dividends; nor were the "B" shares convertible.

Although already well known in the Champaign-Urbana area from years as a contractor, real estate broker, insurance agency owner and securities agent, Snook was also active in civic and church activities. He was a Mason, an active Kiwanian, a volunteer of the Savoy Methodist Church, a leading volunteer with the local Boy Scout Council, a fund raiser for many local charities and involved in a host of other activities. Snook was also in demand and busy on the speaking circuit. News of the formation of a large life insurance company headquartered in Champaign was "big news" for everyone in the community. A local news clipping dated February 12, 1964 in the *News-Gazette* read: *West Point Society to Hear Snook.*

Q.L. Snook had come a long way in a short time indeed. The kid from Bloomington who helped his dad run a feed mill had been honored at the West Point Society for his civic, business and charitable efforts.

Between the November organizational meeting and the end of the year 1964, Snook and the holding company had raised $610,532.70. He had a sales force of fifty-one agents hired within thirty days. Every agent of the company was required to attend a three-day securities course. Q.L. was determined to accomplish his goal.

Snook had also set the board for the Holding Corporation of America. Q.L. Snook was chairman and president; John Howarth, vice president and board member; Kenneth Imig, secretary and board member; Jerome Spector, treasurer and board member; and Richard Peterson, company attorney and board member.

Snook knew that his board was critical to the success of his plan. He had given much thought and time to the selection of the board, and the chemistry that would be created from it. These men, after all, would be responsible for a tremendous amount of cash and the formation of several companies, including the acquisition of several more.

Don Cheatum was elected vice president in charge of sales. Cheatum was a great leader. To be lured away from the Dale Carnegie Institute where Cheatum had earned the honor of "Most Outstanding Associate Sponsor in the World" in 1963, was no small undertaking. Cheatum was also involved in the activities of the Chamber of Commerce and had extensive business contacts throughout Illinois.

John Howarth was a career salesman and was the regional director of a manufacturing firm. He and Snook had been friends for many years. Kenneth Imig was well known among Illinois farmers as the president of the Illinois Farm Advisers Association, a group that assisted farmers throughout the state on a number of legal, economic and political issues. He was a key member for his influence among farmers and his overall knowledge of the industry. Jerome Spector was a business man from New Lenox. Also a contractor and former business owner, Snook admired Spector's financial and business sense. The final member of the board, Richard Peterson, was a Chicago attorney. Peterson was with the firm of Peterson, Bogucki and Bickley.

With Cheatum and Snook both active in recruiting agents, the field grew from a handful of agents at the beginning to over 200 within a matter of months. Newspaper clippings in early 1965 reported that the Holding Corporation America was selling stock shares at a rate of $750,000 a month! By May, the company had over $2,500,000 in cash in the bank and the amount was growing daily. An article in the *Champaign-Urbana Courier* on July 15, 1965 reported that Holding Corporation of America had more than 5,600 stockholders and had just surpassed $3,000,000 in capital in the Champaign National Bank. Snook was quoted as saying that his goal had always been to "build the largest life insurance company in the state in terms of initial capital." He went on to say that, "The response has been fantastic to our stock offering in the first five months. The initial goals of 4,000 stockholders has been greatly surpassed already!" How was he able to accomplish this so quickly? Among many other methods, Snook used his unique referral system.

Topping the financial news section of the *Champaign-Urbana Courier* Financial section on October 7, 1965 was the following article:

Q.L. Snook, president of the Champaign-based Holding Corporation of America, announced Thursday the company's $4 million stock issue had been completely sold after only seven months. Holding Corporation of America was formed to control the soon-to-be-created Thomas Jefferson Life Insurance Company, which will also be based in Champaign. Snook said negotiations were satisfactorily underway for a new building in Champaign to house both Holding Corporation of America and the insurance company. Stock sales in the insurance company will begin after the state grants approval, Snook said. Snook said district offices for the company would be established in Rockford, Peoria, Rock Island, Springfield, Decatur, Chicago, Danville, Bloomington, Quincy and Kankakee.

What must have seemed like a distant dream to many had become a reality in seven months! Snook had wanted to raise $4,000,000 for the holding corporation in its first year, and that ambitious goal had been accomplished. His sales organization and training methods were so thorough that the company stock oversold, resulting in refunds and rejections. In its seven-month march to formation, 7,720 stockholders had invested and purchased stock. Publishers of financial papers in the mid-1960s marveled at the accomplishment, as did many of Snook's stockholders, and even some of the board members.

"I never doubted it could be done," Snook commented with a twinkle in his eye.

True to his original plan, Snook immediately sought approval from the state's insurance commissioner to form Thomas Jefferson Life.

In January 1966 Snook held a meeting with 400 regional stockholders of the Holding Corporation of America to form Thomas Jefferson Life. At the meeting Snook announced that he would offer an additional $4,000,000 of stock to increase capitalization to $6,700,000. The holding corporation was investing $3,250,000 to form the insurance company. With 7,720 stockholders in Holding Corporation of America, Snook saw few problems in raising the $4,000,000 to further capitalize the insurance company. It had always been an integral part of the master plan.

Snook had become such an important cog in the Holding Corporation America and Thomas Jefferson Life plan that the Holding Corporation of America board voted unanimously to take out a policy of "key man" insurance on its founder, Q.L. Snook. The $1,000,000 policy written on Snook's life was the largest single policy ever written by Kentucky Central Life Insurance of Lexington, Kentucky, in its sixty-three year history. HCA was named beneficiary.

"That's when I started looking over my shoulder," Snook quipped about the size of the policy.

The groundwork for selling the life insurance had been laid. Snook had almost 200 agents under contract even before the company was formed. The agents were scattered strategically throughout Illinois, and were already well trained from the Cheatum/Snook securities training school, which had been such a success. With over 7,700 stockholders, Snook and his associates had little doubt that Thomas Jefferson Life would instantly become a tremendous success in Illinois. The licensing process went through without a hitch. Snook had once again done his homework thoroughly.

To house the two newly formed companies, the Holding Corporation of America board decided to purchase the old Masonic Lodge of Champaign, which had fallen into disrepair. Although Snook could easily have picked a less expensive site and project, he had raised money for the Masons, and was a Mason. The building was located at 202 West Hill in Champaign and was completely renovated by the Holding Corporation of America, with Q.L. Snook taking personal charge of the project.

"The building had so much history," Snook said. The four-story building and parking area occupied one-half of a city block and, with its stately columns, had served as the home of Western Star Lodge No. 240, AF&AM of Champaign since 1913, when it was built. Snook called the building "one of the most impressive buildings an insurance company could have as a home office." Although extensive remodeling was needed on the outside and inside of the building, Snook decided to retain the auditorium on the top floor of the building, and remodeled it for the purpose of sales meetings and a conference area.

"When we complete the public offering of our stock," Snook told the *Courier* newspaper on February 20, 1966, which reported the acquisition of the temple, "we will be the largest new life insurance company ever formed in Illinois in terms of initial capitalization." Snook went on to discuss what the business would do for the community. "The community will benefit from the company's growing payroll and the additional business it will bring to town through our conferences and activities."

Snook staffed the newly remodeled home of the Holding Corporation of America and Thomas Jefferson Life with fifteen employees and state-of-the-art IBM office equipment.

In speeches throughout Illinois, Snook promoted the companies. "Last year, approximately thirty percent of the life insurance written in Illinois was written by the eighty-five companies domiciled in Illinois. The rest was written by 300 companies not domiciled in the state. Our philosophy was 'Why can't Illinois people get together, form their own giant company and keep this business in their own state?' That's what we intend to do."

Snook's traveled the state in conjunction with his mission and people responded positively. What he told them made sense. He was impressive in his presentations and his grand business plan was well underway.

Snook's energy and innovation in promoting Thomas Jefferson Life catapulted the company forward.

He used his airplane to fly from office to office, encouraging, promoting, inspiring his agents throughout Illinois. He set up sales contests, offered trips and premiums for sales volume and constantly was recognizing his most successful agents. Promotion and marketing were Snook's strengths. They became his trademark. Although the amount of commission that any agent could make was set by an actuary and approved by the Illinois Insurance Department, Snook took it upon himself to make sure that agents knew it was profitable to sell for Thomas Jefferson Life Insurance Company and Holding Corporation of America, they were constantly recognized, awarded and thanked.

"It is a small thing to do, to thank someone," Snook says, "but lucky for me, the agents weren't getting treated very well by the other companies."

Snook rallied his agents with regular sales meetings that were charged with energy, enthusiasm and opportunities to win premiums, trips and prizes. It brought even the most seasoned sales professionals into his confidence. Regular newsletters to his sales force throughout the state were filled with photos of successful agents, innovative sales ideas, names of new clients and his ever-present high energy.

Throughout his organization, Snook's agents took the same patriotic message into every civic club, political rally and function. It was an integral part of the Snook marketing plan.

One goal of the plan had been to post a profit within the first year of operations of the Holding Corporation of America, and in April 1967, at the second annual meeting of the stockholders of the Holding Corporation of America, Snook announced an incredible pre-tax profit of $149,851.40 for the first year, 1966. His promise was secure. Stockholders would have a profit in their first year of operation.

At the same meeting Snook announced that the Holding Corporation of America had 7,720 shareholders and had *oversold* the $4,000,000 stock offering! The board had to turn would-be investors away. The *Champaign-Urbana News-Gazette* reported the meeting citing, "With its $4,000,000 capitalization, the Holding Corporation of America is the largest of its kind in the history of Illinois at the date of its formation."

On December 10, 1965, Thomas Jefferson Life received a state certificate of authority to do business in the state of Illinois. Having been recently funded with $3,250,000 in cash from its parent company, Holding Corporation of America, Thomas Jefferson Life Insurance Company of America was born. So far, the business plan he had written almost three years earlier was working to perfection.

Although the company could have begun selling insurance as soon as their certificate arrived, Snook was patient. His plan was to offer $4,000,000 in stock, have it completely sold, and then, and only then, start selling insurance. While he had an initial sales force for

Thomas Jefferson Life of almost 200 agents, he wanted to expand it. To take the young company to the top of the insurance sales charts in the state, Snook felt the company needed 500 agents, trained and ready to sell when the stock issue was complete.

Elected to the board of the life insurance company were: Q.L. Snook, chairman of the board and president; Richard Peterson, vice president and legal counsel; Charles Ray, administrative vice president and secretary; Charles Sandage, and Rodger Bliss, directors.

Snook had, once again, personally selected the directors for the life insurance company. Charles Ray was appointed to run the internal operations of the new company. Ray had served in a similar capacity with two Indiana life insurance companies and was extremely knowledgeable about the actuarial and underwriting policies as well as other internal affairs such as finance and staffing. Ray was also selected because he was well known outside of Illinois insurance circles, and even consulted for large insurance companies overseas. Snook had major plans for Thomas Jefferson Life and future acquisitions for the Holding Corporation of America.

Cheatum's talents had already been demonstrated with the hiring of almost 300 agents and the successful training and ensuing stock sale of the Holding Corporation of America. Snook believed that he now needed to shift his focus on insurance and sales training for agents in Thomas Jefferson Life. Cheatum would assume the training responsibility.

Rodger Bliss had long been Q.L.'s friend. A quiet, unassuming man, Bliss had a rare sales talent which many, including Snook, had admired for years.

Charles Sandage was a career educator and close friend of Snook's. As a professor of advertising at the University of Illinois, Dr. Sandage was well-respected throughout the area for having a quick mind and cool head, both of which Snook thought would be needed. Years later in 1993, Sandage would write *Roads to be Taken,* an authoritative text on marketing and advertising and his life story.

Richard Peterson rounded out the board. As an attorney, it had been Peterson who fought the $7,725,000 libel suit brought by Republic Investors Life Insurance Company against Snook. Snook also hired Selmer Dockter as controller of the new company. Dockter had served with Northern Life Insurance Company in North Dakota prior to being hired by Thomas Jefferson Life.

In June of 1966 Snook invited over 100 agents and their families to the new headquarters of Thomas Jefferson Life. The meeting was held for one purpose—to get people motivated! After a brief sales meeting in which Snook explained the many products and services to be offered by Thomas Jefferson Life, the rest of the day was spent in merriment. Snook hosted a delicious picnic buffet for all of the families. Games, prizes and awards were given away all afternoon.

While gaining momentum with the agents, and contracting with new ones every day, the stock offering was going well. Having started on December 10, 1965, by the following December the goal had been reached; over $4,000,000 in cash had been raised through stock sales. The total capitalization of Thomas Jefferson Life was $7,000,000 in cash. While most new life insurance companies operate at a loss for up to ten years after formation, Snook's company would post a profit and give a dividend to its shareholders in the first year of its operation!

In less than two years Q.L. Snook had raised almost $8,000,000 dollars. He had stated that lofty goal when he had met in the basement of his brother Wilbur's home in Bloomington, Illinois, to discuss the idea, and he systematically went out and accomplished it. Never had a life insurance company been so well-funded, well-staffed, and well-positioned to set new records of insurance sales and profits for its investors. Snook hadn't neglected any phase of the operation. He personally oversaw it all. Few entrepreneurs other than Q.L. Snook could have managed such an undertaking.

In November 1966, with 400 agents, wives, stockholders and directors, Snook finally gave the go-ahead to begin selling insurance. Everything was in place. The *Champaign-Urbana Courier* reported the event, saying:

"President Q.L. Snook told the assembled agents to begin selling life insurance policies Tuesday and to set plenty of new records to get the young company off to the best possible start. Snook also reported that capital surplus was almost at $7,000,000 and that not only was Thomas

Jefferson Life the largest capitalized insurance company in Illinois history, but had also set a record for stock distribution to over 15,000 shareholders, all of whom are residents of Illinois. Mr. Snook went on to say that to the best of his knowledge this is the first life insurance company ever to show a profit during its first year, during the stock offering, having had no insurance sales at all!"

Well before a Thomas Jefferson Life board had ever been appointed, Snook had projected that his new company's sales would be $100,000,000 in its first full year of operation. Many might have doubted him then, but no one doubted him now.

During the formation of the Holding Corporation of America and Thomas Jefferson Life, Snook held the full-time position of president of Q.L. Snook Enterprises, and president of the Champaign Securities Company, along with his other companies that had been formed years earlier. He collected no salary from the holding corporation, devoting countless hours in the planning and execution of his elaborate business plan to form both companies. Snook often said that without his secretary, Nora Witt, the two companies might simply have ceased to function during those months of organization. Another valuable secretary was hired later, Linda Hatfield. The women kept Snook's companies organized and running efficiently.

His final goal was to be profitable from the start. From the opening bell, Snook had said he would return a handsome profit from the first year of operations. On February 19, 1967, the *News-Gazette* reported first-year earnings of Thomas Jefferson Life of $150,000. The reason for the unexpectedly large profit was another of Q.L. Snook's ideas. It hadn't been done before in the history of life insurance companies in Illinois.

Snook knew that to be competitive in the insurance business he needed to have a lot more than just money in the bank and agents. Although necessary and helpful, he needed to have a line of products that people simply couldn't get elsewhere. He needed to offer service that customers couldn't get anywhere. So Snook offered his policy holders new products that hadn't been sold in Illinois before.

Snook and his actuary, Ed Peters and Associates, came up with the policy called "The Independence Plan." It was sold as the ideal way to independence through life insurance. Eight and a half months were spent to perfect the policy and it was impressive, to say the least.

The "Independence Plan," although well-known today in the insurance industry, was a revolutionary concept that Snook and his actuarial firm advanced in the mid-1960s. It skyrocketed sales and earnings to new levels in the insurance industry and got the attention of every competitor in the state, and many others throughout the country. No one was selling this type of policy. While his competitors studied the "Independence Plan," Snook was busy with his more than 300 agents statewide selling it.

With such planning and execution evident at his companies, the Holding Corporation of America and

Thomas Jefferson Life, it seemed that Snook was destined to rewrite sales history for life insurance in Illinois, perhaps even America. With his first year behind him, Snook had already made a profit for his investors. But Q.L. Snook was well beyond the first year in his planning, well before the year even began. He was researching more innovative insurance products to create and sell, and spent a lot of time traveling to seek out other companies who offered their policy holders innovative and unique policies. Being the visionary that he was, Snook couldn't put up his feet and enjoy his success to date. He didn't have time for it. For him, the love was in the chase and the planning, not in the capture and ultimate reward of the venture.

Snook was already looking at insurance companies to purchase in other states, companies that he could buy at the right price, build with his level of motivation, training skills and fresh ideas: companies that had much going for them but lacking sufficient capital. He had plenty of it and knew first-hand how to raise more.

Thomas Jefferson Indemnity Company was the creation of Q.L. Snook and his longtime friend, Rodger Bliss. Serving as officers along with Q.L. Snook, chairman of the board, were Charles Ray, president; James Bliss, secretary; Charles Sandage, treasurer; and Joe Frank, director.

Even his board of directors and close friends couldn't have imagined how far in the future Snook was planning. They couldn't know that he already had a plan for expansion into every state in the country.

Snook was convinced, and rightfully so, that the key to rapid growth in other states was through acquisition, not waiting out the protracted, frustrating process of insurance licensing. The company had the money. He had the skill and insight. He was poised now to build the largest insurance company in North America. He had convinced the directors and they had become believers. Q.L. Snook had a way of making people believe in him. He had a way of selling his dream so that other people could share his excitement, his dream. Snook had already envisioned the expansion of the company into all fifty states. It was only a matter of execution now—find the right companies, purchase them at the right price and build them on the principles, resources and skills that the companies possessed. For Snook's part, he was already researching something called ATM banking, a revolutionary way to accomplish drive-through banking transactions. He believed it represented the future and would be a growth industry in the next decade or two. He also was researching cable television, and believed that there was tremendous knowledge and entertainment that cable could bring area residents. He began a long process of trying to bring cable television to Champaign, and despite many groups that fought him, he believed this to be another growth industry that he should involve himself in.

Snook began to take his inspired ideas to the board and thought they would agree with him enthusiastically. But something slowly began to change.

Instead of embracing his ideas with excitement, certain board members began to close their minds to his thinking. Perhaps they were focusing their eyes on the fat prize that lay in assets. Millions in cash can turn even the most ardent purist into something else. Often dumbfounded at certain board members' attitudes about his growth plans, Snook began to feel concern.

Although his business plan had gone off without a hitch, he hadn't counted on something far less predictable than business cycles and selling patterns—human nature. The Holding Corporation of America might have been destined to be the holder of many companies, some not even related to insurance. That was a part of Snook's plan. Thomas Jefferson Life was to become the largest seller of insurance in America. That also was a part of Snook's plan.

Snook would soon be embroiled in a battle far tougher than the Republic Investors proxy fight and lawsuit, with those who had envious eyes on the riches of the company's assets. While he needed to cast his eyes carefully on those closest to him, he was traveling far afield to find the right companies to buy and increase shareholder values. Q.L. Snook might have been wiser to watch his own house. In retrospect, he would also have been wise to consider another adage like those his father often repeated: "God defend me from my friends; from my enemies I can defend myself." The ensuing battle over how to spend their millions would eventually bring the entire company to the brink of disaster, and Snook to a new awareness. His ultimate challenge still lay ahead of him.

When it no longer fits,
it's time to walk away

The 1965 Annual Report of the Holding Corporation of America printed this about their president, founder and chairman of the board:

....It has been said that, "A successful corporation is the lengthened shadow of one man's vision and purpose," and thus it is in the case of Q.L. Snook.

....Inspired by his guidance, leadership, and enthusiasm, the Holding Corporation of America is now a reality, an organization of devoted personnel joined into a major force of readiness and capability.

With funding of $4,000,000 in cash and almost 8,000 shareholders, the company seemed destined to become one of America's largest corporations. The 1965 Annual Report concluded with these comments:

It all began with an honorable idea, promulgated by honorable men, dedicated to honorable methods, without deviation from principles to achieve a common purpose that shall result in unending success. It all began with one, carrying a message to a few, progressing to thousands whose faith and confidence made possible a record achievement of a capitalization of $4,000,000 accomplished in record time with the cooperation of all...and at a profit.

.....To this end we are forever dedicated.

As it began, the Holding Corporation of America was the catalyst for a new life insurance company, Thomas Jefferson Life. With plenty of money, many agents, and innovative policies to sell to thousands of investors already, Thomas Jefferson Life was destined to become a giant in the life insurance industry. Snook appointed six regional directors and started a national search for a qualified director of sales, then called a director of agencies. An issue of 800,000 shares of common stock in Thomas Jefferson Life raised an additional $3,500,000 after commissions. Snook took another seven months to prepare before he authorized the company to sell its first policy. Every aspect of the company's anticipated performance was analyzed and planned.

When sales commenced they were immediate and strong, as anticipated. With the planning of the Holding Corporation of America and Thomas Jefferson Life complete, Snook began to implement the next phase of his master plan; namely, to find profitable and solid life insurance companies in other states to acquire.

In early 1967, after months of negotiations, Snook and Thomas Jefferson Life Insurance Company purchased one hundred percent of the stock of the powerful Western Life Insurance Company of St. Louis, Missouri. Western Life had been selling insurance for seventy-one years and was a solid, reputable company licensed to do business in Missouri, Illinois, Arkansas and Kansas. It was just the mix that Snook and the directors of Thomas Jefferson Life Insurance Company had been looking for. Western Life's $65,000,000 insurance in force added to Thomas Jefferson Life's $16,000,000 written at the time of the purchase for a combined $80,000,000 in sales.

The purchase of Western Life placed Thomas Jefferson Life in the top forty percent of all life insurance companies in Illinois in insurance in force, and among the top twenty percent of Illinois life companies with total assets of over $10,500,000. Snook's plan was working well.

With Western Life aboard, the company continued to prosper. By the end of the fourth year in business, Thomas Jefferson Life had shown steady and impressive growth. Following an unprecedented first- year profit without selling a policy, Thomas Jefferson Life posted a profit of $16,000 in its second year, and $94,000 in profit in 1968, its third year. With the addition of Western Life the company's profits soared in 1969 to $300,000, or a 220 percent increase over 1968. It had been a truly great year. The directors in 1969 stayed the same for Thomas Jefferson Life: Snook, Ray, Bliss, Peterson and Sandage. At the annual meeting Snook recognized his President's Club for 1969: Harlan Bliss, Tony Kahn, Jerry O'Connor, Jim Scanlon, Burford Tummelson, Ladell Tittsworth, Verle Burhenn and Ron Smith. All were $1,000,000 producers or better. Harlan Bliss led the company in production with over $3,000,000 in sales and earned the coveted position as chairman of the President's Club.

But by early 1970 there were problems brewing internally in the company. Members of both boards of the Holding Corporation of America and Thomas Jefferson Life were in an ever-increasing confrontation with Snook's plan for the company. Snook wished to enlarge the empire and purchase other companies, but with each new proposal to the Holding Corporation board, Snook was being turned down. His innovative ideas of expanding beyond the realm of insurance were hotly contested in board meetings. Snook spent months in complicated negotiations for a bank to purchase, trying to bring cable television to Champaign, as well as many other projects, only to be voted down on all the projects except for the cable TV company by the grumbling Holding Corporation of America board of directors.

Ledger assets for Thomas Jefferson Life and Western Life amounted to over $13,000,000. Holding Corporation of America was worth another $4,000,000. Thomas Jefferson Life doubled its net profit from 1969 to 1970 and posted a $220,000 net profit. But Western Life began to falter in 1970. The amount of insurance in force dropped by almost $6,000,000 from 1969 to 1970 and profits fell. Directors of Thomas Jefferson Life looked to Snook's inability to hire and keep key personnel as a possible cause. Snook adamantly denied it, saying that the focus of hiring was a combined responsibility and, eventually, they would find the right leaders. The battles were never heard by employees or stockholders, but differences between Snook and the directors of both companies continued to mount.

Although Snook was shaken by these internal pressures, he didn't buckle. In fact, he strengthened his resolve to continue to lead the company in the direction he had originally and very successfully planned. While he knew that his agents were being provided "inside information" about board discussions, he couldn't be sure where the "leak" was coming from. It was alarming, however.

Board meetings were being called often and frequently erupted in arguments.

While a showdown became imminent, the Thomas Jefferson Life board decided to call in outside assistance to find the root of the problems at Thomas Jefferson Life. With Snook's reluctant approval, the board employed an independent business management consulting firm to make a study of the management problems and recommend a solution. The idea seemed to be a sound decision. Supporters of Snook and his leadership, who composed the vast majority of the company and several directors, believed the study would confirm that Snook's leadership and management ability were solid and that "other rats in the woodpile" might be found. Even Snook supported the study, knowing that he had been fair, honest and had the best interests of the stockholders, policy holders, agents and employees in mind. He was sure that the study would bear that out and the dissension within the company would come to an end.

(Charles Sandage provided a copy of the confidential report by Booz, Allen, Hamilton during the course of writing this book to the author.) The report is restricted to officers and board members of Holding Corporation of America and Thomas Jefferson Life Insurance Company of America.

Although few in number, and often impossible to name, foes of Snook welcomed the report as well. They hoped that the study would examine his management style and find fault with his long-range plan. They believed that if any impropriety were found, the report would conclude that Snook was the cause of the company's problems.

Everyone hoped that the consulting firm would put an end to the upper management problems and that the company could see clearly its future once again. In a forceful move, Snook directed the boards of the Holding Corporation of America and Thomas Jefferson Life, that if the report came back recommending no change of president and leadership, that they would stop the bickering, remove the opposition to his decisions and give the reins of the company back to him. He concluded that if they couldn't do that, then any dissenters should resign their positions and leave the company.

After the report was read, Thomas Jefferson Life director C.H. Sandage, who had secured the consulting group and had facilitated the project, looked to Snook for his reaction. Snook responded that the report was probably accurate in its assessment of management problems and faults. He maintained however, that every company, especially emerging companies, has management challenges. But they were just that, challenges and problems, not just cause for him to step down and threaten the entire future of the company and the trust placed in him from stockholders. *He had committed no illegal act while founding and running the company.* There wasn't even a hint of any impropriety or wrongdoing. If anything, Snook argued, he had probably been too permissive regarding the wishes of other board members, who perhaps had hidden agendas other than the benefit of the stockholders, policy holders, agents and employees!

Snook agreed with the findings to a certain extent. New business written, particularly in Western Life, was trending downward. New business sales in Thomas Jefferson Life, however had enjoyed a steady growth pattern since its formation, and were exceeding industry norms, even in the recessionary times they were in. A new plan for Western Life needed to be put into place, but that was a matter that could be easily resolved.

As for the turnover of agency management and key personnel, Snook again conceded that the four or five men who had occupied these key positions had left for a variety of justifiable reasons, not an inability to work with the president. He cited the case of one of his sales directors, who had been a qualified candidate they had hired to be director of agencies. On a routine check it was found that he had falsified his application and he resigned. Another qualified man was hired, stayed a month and was successfully recruited by a competitor. Others came and followed for just cause, Snook argued. To the charge that he "couldn't delegate authority properly" to these key management positions, Snook responded by saying that because of the high turnover they had experienced, he was reluctant to delegate complete authority, and stayed very close to agency operations, including sales meetings, training, recruitment and other agency management functions. He argued that because of his ultimate concern due to turnover, his efforts should be praised, not criticized.

Snook largely agreed that the Holding Corporation of America and Thomas Jefferson Life were still "finding themselves" as a new company and that the transition period between startup and a smooth operation was incomplete. But again, he pointed out that he had developed and implemented a three-day mandatory training program for new agents that was conducted by one of the best trainers in the country. All agents were thoroughly familiarized with Thomas Jefferson Life policies, sales philosophy and, especially, the new insurance lines that Snook had personally overseen and put in place. As for market planning, Snook took stronger offense. He pointed out that he had done an exhaustive amount of market analysis, studying every major successful life insurance company in the country, and likewise, every failing company. He had spent a lifetime profiling the Illinois market and knew his territory quite well.

As to the matter of acquisition and the report's criticism of their record on mergers and acquisitions, Snook argued that he wouldn't take responsibility for that. He had spent an inordinate amount of time in studying possible acquisitions, seeking several opportunities for the Holding Corporation of America board to approve. His search included several banks, an active desire to bring in cable television, several insurance firms and even a new idea for the time, drive-in banking. The board, he argued, rejected all but the cable television company, preferring to stay in a "slow-growth mode" even with the tremendous capitalization that Snook had accomplished. Snook agreed with the report's findings that they should have acquired more companies, according to Snook's own acquisition plan, but the fault clearly was an inactive board.

Snook also agreed that enthusiasm and morale in the company had slipped. He directed his gaze at the board of directors and asked them how it was that information discussed in this room was being spread to agents throughout the state almost before the secretaries could type up the company's minutes? How could enthusiasm and morale for the product drop after he had introduced new and lucrative insurance products for agents to sell? These products were selling, and agents were making more money than they could have prior to Thomas Jefferson Life's new product line.

Snook argued that morale was being undermined by others, for their own private reasons. For himself, he would not succumb to temptations of huge cash reserves. He would not panic and buy companies without thorough examination or due diligence. Difficulties in the boardroom need not, and should not, be communicated to employees and agents in the field. "Someone," he argued with passion, "might be trying to undermine the company's morale," but it certainly was not he.

Q.L. had many allies within HCA and Thomas Jefferson Life, despite the inner turmoil there. Most people who were acquainted with Snook at the time knew him as a man of passion, energy and enthusiasm. They knew him to be above reproach, honest in all his business dealings. He ran a tight ship, however, as president of the company, he had a responsibility to his stockholders, policy holders, agents and employees. But should this be a reason that he should step down, giving the reins of the company to an outsider? Given the fact that morale might be low and enthusiasm waning, Snook felt that these problems could be solved. "Focus on the solutions," he cited, "not the problems."

The Booz Allen Hamilton report cited the major problems of Holding Corporation of America and Thomas Jefferson Life were organizational in nature. Snook argued that if this were so, then the board should roll up their sleeves and correct the problems, one at a time, following logic and good judgement. Where they were lacking in organization, they could implement a new plan, establish new goals and generate more energy among the staff. He also stated that organization for a relatively new company was often the last mechanism in place following a successful startup. He also identified several areas where the organization was in place, higher than industry standards, such as training, licensing, and new product development.

With every counterpoint that Snook offered, he ended his interrogatives with the same closing argument. "These problems and challenges are resolvable. It is not necessary for me to resign." Q.L. argued that this could open the door for outsiders who might misuse the company for selfish reasons, leading the company in a wrong direction and possibly even to dissolution in the future, which eventually did happen. He maintained that the problems as they had been reported by Booz Allen & Hamilton would still be in place even if he resigned.

Snook felt that if worse came to even worse, that he could win control of the company through a proxy fight. He had, at the time, forty-one percent control of the company, however the idea of a proxy fight bothered him immensely. That would be expensive, and perhaps not in the best interest of his shareholders. The proxy fight could cost as much as $500,000. Sure he could win it, but the company treasury would be crippled. Those who opposed Snook would still be there.

Mired in mistrust and controversy, the board was like a hung jury. Several deficiencies in operations were discovered and highlighted. Snook directed his efforts at correcting those deficiencies and for a time, the breach seemed to heal. Trying to build company morale in recessionary times, Snook was even named "Boss of the Year" in 1972, a prestigious honor considering the size of the Champaign-Urbana area. Although there were smiles all around, the trouble had not gone away, and would flare up again.

The recessionary economy of the early 1970s was hurting the saturated insurance market. Thomas

Jefferson Life was no exception. Snook and the board were unable to turn Western Life around and the company continued to decline. Surprising for the times, however, Thomas Jefferson Life was doing reasonably well, in comparison with other life insurance companies. Ever the motivator, Snook had monthly, and, at times, even weekly sales meetings, reiterating the benefits of Thomas Jefferson Life and the need for discipline, drive and enthusiasm. His message was being heard less and less. Hostility on the Holding Corporation of America and Thomas Jefferson Life boards existed.

Early in the 1970s the board entertained the idea of selling Western Life. The directors had agreed not to sell the company for less than $2,000,000. When a Cuban buyer became interested, he inquired how the securities held in vaults to insure claims worked. Snook grew suspicious of his strong interest in the securities rather than in the company. Later, he found out the man was wanted by the FBI for securities theft!

In early 1974, the Holding Corporation of America board found a small Chicago- based insurance company owned by Victor Sayyah. Snook personally went to meet with him to discuss the opportunity of purchasing Sayyah's company, which was a very small company. Negotiations began and in time, Victor Sayyah's style and charm began to win over several board members with the thought that Sayyah might have the experience, enthusiasm and money to underwrite a buyout of Snook and perhaps could be the man they had been searching for to lead the company.

In the end, Snook reluctantly agreed to sell. While he could have demanded a high price for his stock, he did not. He accepted "book value" for his stock, which was the same value as any stockholder would receive. The total was valued at just over $1,000,000. He certainly could have held out for a higher price, and doubtless, the board would probably have agreed, but Snook was fair, even to the last.

C.H. Sandage was the chief negotiator for the company in these matters, and was appointed a member of the Holding Corporation of America board and eventually became chairman of the Holding Corporation of America and Thomas Jefferson Life boards. He had placed his full confidence in Victor Sayyah to lead the company and arranged suitable terms for Sayyah to purchase most of Snook's controlling interest.

Q.L. Snook sold his interests in both companies and fully divested himself from the Holding Corporation of America and Thomas Jefferson Life. Neither company would thrive, however.

For Q.L. Snook, there would be no other grand business endeavors. He swallowed his pride. He had lost his greatest business creation, at the hands of men he had trusted. While Snook would go on to build a fortune in real estate holdings in Illinois and Deltona, Florida, his days in the world of corporate finance ended when he sold his interests in the Holding

Corporation of American and Thomas Jefferson Life Insurance Company of America.

In October 1996, the merged companies of Thomas Jefferson Life Insurance Company of America and the Holding Corporation of America, now known as I.C.H., filed for chapter 11 bankruptcy protection. Q.L. Snook sold all his interests in the companies in November 1974. As this book is going to press, the future of these companies is being determined in legal proceedings.

Comments

I knew Mr. Snook as a landlord for approximately a year. He continues to be a friend. I first met him in June of 1994. I had just moved my family to Champaign-Urbana. I responded to an ad in the local paper from Mr. Snook about a house. He struck me as a quiet, reticent man, someone who bases decisions to a large extent on personal perceptions and analysis rather than on an attempt to read what others think is right. I was also impressed with the houses that Mr. Snook built. The garages were oversize, not something you would see in a tract home, but much appreciated. The layout of our house was more like those of Florida than the Midwest and the amenities were a cut above what I would have expected. Mr. Snook and his wife are religious people and possess a strong moral compass. They brought an old-fashioned sense of decency and decorum, a kind of refreshing perspective that is somewhat rare. We are proud to count the Snooks among our friends.
Chris Youngworth, Champaign, Ill.

As vice president of sales for the Deltona Corporation, I entered into a franchise agreement with "Q" in the early 1960s to represent us in the Champaign, Illinois, area in the sale of homes, home sites, commercial and industrial properties in our Florida communities. "Q" was eminently successful and a top producer among franchisees of similar-sized territories. He was extremely well organized and one of the very best salesmen I have ever known, among many hundreds in my 40-plus years in the real estate profession.

180

Indeed, on numerous occasions I utilized his great talents as a featured speaker at our annual National Conventions of Franchised Representatives. As a consequence of this exposure, other franchisees privately sought his wise counsel to improve their own performances. I regard him as entrepreneurial in every respect and cannot imagine him failing in anything he undertakes to do.

Neil E. Bahr, Vice Chairman,
The Deltona Corporation, Miami, Florida

The following letter was written August 8, 1973, by George E. Hunt, Jr., CPA with PEER, HUNT AND CURZON to Q.L. Snook:

Dear Quentin,

*Have received from you and your secretary, Linda Hatfield, several flyers on fringe benefits for executives. I know that you constantly desire to "learn" but if there is anyone who rose from a poor teacher to a successful executive, you are it. **You** should be sending out the flyers, not receiving them.*

Just last night, I went to the Rotary "corn boil" and the discussion came to the impossibility today to accumulate because of the tax laws. I cited you as the fallacy of this statement—hard worker and thinker—willing to work all hours—set goals—and willing to assume risks.

People always ask me—how's TJ doing. I say great and growing—because an honest man started it and is still at the controls.

Very truly yours,
George E. Hunt, Jr.

5
THE JOY
OF GIVING

A time to reflect

Q.L. Snook was fifty-one years old when he left the companies he had formed ten years earlier. While he had offers to sell his stock for nearly twice what he ultimately sold for, Snook sold his stock in the Holding Corporation of America and Thomas Jefferson Life at book value for both companies. It had been worth over $2,000,000. He sold at book value, the same value as every shareholder could. This was not a premium. It has been said, "He had sold at a very high price for his corporate position." How could this be true? Q.L. had offers of over twice book value that Snook refused because that would be unfair to the other shareholders.

Immediately following his departure, Snook took some needed time off. He got involved with more civic and volunteer activities and breathed deeply again, away from the pressures at Thomas Jefferson Life and the Holding Corporation of America. He resumed his interest in real estate.

Although he considered it, he never again would form another company. The Holding Corporation of America experience was too painful. He had done all he could to save the company from the hands of men who cared much less about his stockholders and his dream; but in the end, he watched it all go down, just as he predicted it would. One by one, his closest friends and allies left the companies.

Snook just couldn't dwell on it, however. What purpose would it serve? He had to move on. And move on he did. Q.L. returned to his love of home building and real estate.

Either through developing raw land or purchasing existing houses, Snook built ownership in real estate in Illinois and Deltona. He also owns and manages an impressive number of properties in Illinois. He is a caring landlord of his properties. All of his properties are maintained in top condition. His enthusiasm and spirit are admired by almost every tenant he has.

Although his life made a radical turn in 1974, Snook's passion for planning and executing any project never varied. With intense drive, scrupulous honesty and a zest for every moment of the day, Snook chose to go it alone after 1974. His land and property holdings he manages himself.

His love for service to others did not change either after 1974; in fact, Snook got more involved in various activities.

"When I was twenty-four, I made a promise to myself that if I ever became successful (I had no idea what that meant) I would give as much as I could back to my community."

And so he truly began.

He served as international delegate for Kiwanis, and involved himself in many, many Kiwanis' projects in Illinois and Deltona. He became actively involved in building campaigns in United Methodist Churches in both Illinois and Florida, and even donated homes and property for church use. Drawing on his rich bank of experience, Snook also became active in SCORE,

Service Corps of Retired Executives. Forever the teacher, Snook began to counsel small-business owners in a variety of fields, assisting them with business plans, setup, marketing and sales strategies and follow-through. He never accepted any money for these efforts, but did it all for the love of business and a deep, abiding respect for his fellow man.

Snook served on the board of the McKinley YMCA in Champaign, applying his varied business principles to better organize the volunteer efforts of raising money to build a fitness center. He believes that service organizations, including churches, need to run more by the principles of sound business than many do, and has been outspoken at times about this philosophy. Some have heeded his advice, and many have not.

He became heavily involved with the Boy Scout Council and served as Sustaining Membership Chairman, raising money for them. His efforts to the Scouts earned him the award given to volunteers, the Silver Beaver Award.

If he were asked, he almost always would say yes. It was his way, his spirit, his desire to see others succeed.

A Legion of Honor

Kiwanis International began on January 21, 1915 in Detroit, Michigan. A year later the Kiwanis Club of Hamilton, Ontario, Canada was chartered. From both of these clubs Kiwanis International grew rapidly until Kiwanis clubs can now be found in every part of the world. With members in seventy-eight nations, Kiwanis members and the works they do, have a great impact on local communities. Kiwanis members are active or retired professionals, and clubs comprise both men and women. Kiwanis club members often get involved in just about anything that is good for the community and the nation. Today, programs like UNICEF are being funded by Kiwanis. In fact, Kiwanis launched a worldwide service project in 1994 to help eradicate iodine deficiency disorders, a project funded with over $75,000,000.

The motto of Kiwanis is "We Build," and no service organization could have had a stronger influence on young Q.L. Snook than a club with a motto designed for a builder.

The creed of Kiwanis International are words that Snook has personally adopted:

To give primacy to the human and spiritual, rather than to the material values of life.

To encourage the daily living of the Golden Rule in all human relationships.

To promote the adoption and the application of higher social, business, and professional standards.

To develop, by precept and example, a more intelligent, aggressive, and serviceable citizenship.

To provide through Kiwanis Clubs, a practical means to form enduring friendships, to render altruistic service, and to build better communities.

To co-operate in creating and maintaining that sound public opinion and high idealism which make possible the increase of righteousness, justice, patriotism and good will.

Snook first heard of Kiwanis through family friend and relative, Hartwell Howard. Howard had been a Kiwanis member for years and told Q.L. of all the activities they were involved. If it was good enough for Hartwell Howard, it certainly was good enough for Q.L. Snook!

Upon an invitation from Howard, Snook attended his first Kiwanis meeting in Champaign and was forever hooked.

"I really developed a hunger for Kiwanis. In fact, I think I was *starving* for it."

Kiwanis satisfied something in Snook that he hadn't had much time for previously, the ability to give time and talents to others, especially kids.

A negative experience in the Christian Science Church had left Snook without a place to give something back to his community. Snook cites the reason for the falling out was over "dues paying" to the church. He didn't like the way they handled their dues collections. While church had been important to Snook and his family, Q.L. stayed away from any organized church for fifteen years. It just didn't play any part in his life, although his wife and family often were in attendance. He remained home with the baby so the older children could be in Sunday school with their mother assisting as teacher.

Snook's involvement with Kiwanis became an important activity for him. He rarely will ever miss a Kiwanis meeting. Always with a tremendous appetite of giving to others, Snook found an outlet in Kiwanis. It became his tithing ground, both for money and time.

The initiation into the Kiwanis Club wasn't automatic. They were taking only two members of any one profession when Snook applied. He even had to alter his profession slightly to gain acceptance!

"Kiwanis is not just a social club," Snook says. He says that committees are formed within the structure of the club, and each committee takes on projects to oversee, develop, build or operate. With a heavy emphasis on youth, Snook's club was heavily involved with Boy Scouts, Girl Scouts, and Boys Clubs, to name a few. The group also got involved with recognition for teachers, coaches and leaders of youth. Often this was done with recognition plaques or even recognition dinners. The local Champaign Club holds annual honors banquets for University of Illinois athletes and staff. The group has a welfare fund set up for families or people who are in need, or lose a home or business to fire, flood or storm.

One of Snook's early projects was a building project at Camp Kiwanis, a camp for Girl Scouts that was about ten miles from Champaign. Snook's enthusiasm for the project won approval among his peers.

"I was so eager to do this, it was like making a $1,000 a minute!"

The initial project Snook oversaw was the construction of a dispensary building for the camp, a major project in which he took a lot of time to personally work. Snook eagerly assisted Kiwanis in raising money for the project. With a hammer in hand, he led a group of volunteers to erect the building, all in Snook's customary *high standard of quality.*

Following the dispensary building, Snook supervised the fund raising and building of a dining hall for the camp. "Children are priority one with Kiwanis," Snook says. They had no money to build the dining hall, but Snook teamed up with a banker friend and fellow Kiwanian named Mr. Lewis Clausen. Together they successfully approached the Illinois Lumber Manufacturing Company to provide the trusses. Snook laid the foundation, and Clausen and his bank funded the project. The whole building went up in a hurry.

"I was so grateful and thankful to be a part of that club," Snook says modestly. "I really grew to enjoy Kiwanis, still do! The involvement with Kiwanis brings you out. It helps you do things that are beyond yourself." There is much to be gained for getting *beyond oneself,* and for Snook, it was the avenue he had been waiting for. He was the first to volunteer, and despite heavy business schedules and commitments, Q.L. always found the time.

191

During his early years with the Kiwanis, Snook gave more time than money; after all, it wasn't right to take money away from his family when he had family obligations! His business was young. Time was something Snook gave to the Kiwanis projects in Champaign. He always loved doing it.

A club secretary, O.O. Smith had impressed upon a young Snook, a new member, that attendance was vital. He shouldn't miss a meeting if he were to be a true member. That went deep with Snook. Often he drove up to twenty-five miles for a make up, if he did miss a meeting. It became a habit with him. In 1998, Q.L. Snook will have been a member of Kiwanis for fifty years. He has had perfect attendance from his first year on! Smith's stern warning about casual attendance was something Snook never forgot!

Kiwanis became Snook's passion. Attendance in Kiwanis and involvement were commandments to him. He was taught in Kiwanis, "Never to say no," and he rarely did. Community service through Kiwanis became precious to him.

The club elected Snook four times to be their international delegate to take part in national, and even international, concerns. The first election to this post was in 1955 and Snook traveled to Cleveland, Ohio, at his own expense, to represent the local club. The conventions that were held by Kiwanis were important. Votes were taken on policy, as well as on their position regarding social and moral issues. Later he attended Kiwanis conventions in Arizona, Louisiana, and even an international convention in Vienna, Austria, that was organized with the help of E.M. "Turk" Edwards, past lieutenant governor of the Illinois-Iowa Kiwanis district.

It was the Kiwanis Clubs taking the lead over other civic clubs to welcome women into their ranks. With the policy changed, Snook took it upon himself to offer introduction and membership to the first woman inducted in the Champaign Kiwanis club.

"I saw so many capable women who had so much to give," Snook says. "Our purpose is service; it has nothing to do with men or women." While Q.L. was president of the local club, the Kiwanianne Club started for all women. When co-ed members were admitted to Kiwanis International , the Kiwaniannes terminated the Champaign-Urbana club.

Membership into a service organization like Kiwanis isn't something that Q.L. takes lightly. He offers the same advice for others.

"Don't get involved if you don't have the time, or aren't willing to give the time," Snook says emphatically. "You don't benefit, the club doesn't benefit and the community doesn't benefit."

That's Q.L.'s philosophy on most things. *Do it with all your heart, mind and soul, or just don't do it!*

Snook's philosophy on recruiting others into service organizations is a bit unique as well. He requires new members to take an oath, even if Kiwanis does not.

"It is an honor and a privilege to be a part of this. I look for the right qualifications in people, and tell them that they might not qualify for our club!"

Snook feels people need to be committed. It is the minimum requirement. Not for a month or two, but "join forever," Snook counsels.

Involvement in a service organization is vital to the well- being of any business person, according to Snook. He says it allows people to "go beyond themselves," by helping others and thus, find meaning and purpose in their lives other than in the pursuit of money and success.

Snook's involvement with the Champaign Kiwanis Club was like that: full of enthusiasm, commitment and purpose. For example, in 1976 the club was approached by the local Girls Club. They were an active organization involving many girls in Champaign, but had no place to meet and no money. Snook took on the project with his usual vigor and zeal, and volunteered to lead a Kiwanis committee to look into the matter. After a brief meeting with local leaders of the Girls Club, Snook quickly saw the need.

First, he went out and recruited key business leaders to serve on his committee. He hand-picked the team needed to get the job done and convinced them all of the tremendous importance and need for their immediate and resolute involvement. He wasn't looking for names to fill a roster. As usual, Snook needed "movers and shakers" to accomplish his mission.

On his committee Snook recruited an architect, a lawyer named Bill Evans, a general contractor, and a banker. "Go beyond yourselves," Snook challenged them. "We need to build a home for these kids!"

With Snook in command, the committee became *greatly energized.* No one doubted that these girls would get a home built for them, a place where they could meet and the values that they needed in their future lives could be taught to them.

Q.L. states, "We weren't just interested in finding them a place to meet. We needed to build with vision. We wanted to build them a place that they could use to recruit every girl in town, a place that would last and fulfill their mission for years to come!"

Snook also realized that the organization of the local Girls Club also needed to be overhauled. They also needed to *see his vision for their future.*

"The Girls Club didn't have much organization, just a few parents. But we knew that when their kids grew up they would leave. The club needed organization and leadership. If we were going to build them a home for the future, then they also needed leadership that could take them into the future."

Many of the same people that Snook had recruited to build the home of the Girls Club of Champaign, also followed Snook into the leadership of the club itself. With full blessings and welcome from the core group of parents in the program, Snook and his team helped them set up bylaws, a mission statement, goals, a recruitment plan, solid program ideas, more leadership, more parents, recruitment nights to involve other girls and a program for all the local elementary schools in the area. Before the concept *Build it and they will come* became popular, Snook was living it.

Snook wasn't interested in buying an existing house. The house needed to be built just for the Girls Club, designed for that purpose. Thus the need for the architect. Q.L. needed to find the right lot in which to build the house, and found it on a large corner lot in the heart of the community. The lot needed to have room to expand the house. It needed to have room for these children to play and to learn. He had a vision in mind.

Once Q.L. found the lot, the Champaign-Urbana Kiwanis Club purchased it. He gave his passionate presentation to the owner of the lot, telling him how important it was that these girls have a home. How good he would feel if he would part with it, possibly even without charge! He told the man that the newspapers would write a feature story about the project and that the owner would be recognized, written about, and perhaps even honored with a dedication from the Girls Club for years to come.

Not surprisingly, the lot was acquired!

With the architect busily creating the design at no expense, Snook found low-interest money from the banker on his committee to build and finance the house. He got lumber at cost from the builder. Soon the foundation was being poured, the walls were going up and the house was taking shape as the future home of the Champaign Girls Club.

The local newspaper marveled at the size of the house and the planning which had gone into it. *Do a project with all of your heart, soul and mind* Snook believes, or don't do it all.

The house was soon completed and dedicated. Snook made sure the owner of the lot and all of his committee members received the recognition when the papers came to report on the project all in the name of Kiwanis. He made sure that readers of the article would also become enthused about it and bring their girls to join. He had an organization already formed and in place to welcome the children with an exciting and worthwhile program, all under the best leadership in town.

He personally accepted little recognition for his efforts. Instead, he gave it to others. He didn't need the plaque and the honorable mention. He knew what he had done. He had built a home, a program, a leadership base, for girls of the area to enjoy for years to come. That was recognition enough for him.

"You have to see the need," Snook advises, "and then react to it. You can't wait. The opportunity may pass you by and be lost forever."

There is wisdom in those words: *you can't wait, the opportunity may pass you by and be lost forever.*

The Champaign, Illinois Girls Club program became a model for the entire organization, nationwide. It grew and prospered and is still prospering today, almost twenty years later, all because of the vision of one man who *couldn't wait, lest the opportunity to help pass him by, and be lost forever.*

Throughout Q.L. Snook's forty-eight years in Kiwanis, he has continued to make this sort of difference. On projects too numerous to mention,

Snook has taken the lead, or been a part of a team of others to build, to make a difference, to leave behind a *solid thing of lasting good.* It isn't membership in this service group that is important to Snook, it is *involvement.* It is passion, spirit and commitment and the willingness to help others, to *go beyond ourselves.*

Without the insight of these Kiwanians of Champaign, Illinois, the Girls Club house might never have been built. The organization for the club might never have been formed.

Snook feels that Americans have passed by those opportunities too often, and for too long. He maintains that most people aren't *going beyond themselves*, but are too focused on themselves. Can one person make a difference? He believes with all his heart and soul that one person can make a difference in the lives of many. In the case of the Girls Club of Champaign, Illinois, there have been hundreds of children who went through their program since that house was built.

Could people survive without a house for teaching and nurturing children? The answer is obviously yes, but, because of the efforts of Snook and people like him all across America who see an opportunity, act upon it, and build something of lasting value, our communities are better places to live, and our citizens and future citizens are better people.

Snook maintains that this is what Kiwanis is all about: helping build a better person, a better community and a better world, one project and one person at a time.

The story of the Girls Club has been repeated many times in organizations like the Scouts, homes for battered women and children, and others. Through the Kiwanis, men and women are able to *go beyond themselves*, serving others with spirit and enthusiasm, and becoming more and more fulfilled as they go. Snook maintains that this is what giving is all about: becoming quality human beings and living the human experience to the maximum. The gift becomes almost incidental. It is in the act of giving that we often gain the most lasting gratification of all.

1997 is the forty-ninth year anniversary of Q.L. Snook's service to the Kiwanis organization. He maintains active membership today; in fact, his passion is stronger than ever. For his service, Q.L. Snook has been awarded their tribute, the Legion of Honor.

The gift of family

Snook was also able to spend more time with his children after leaving the Holding Corporation of America and Thomas Jefferson Life.

His oldest, Quentin Laurence, Jr. (Larry), was born on August 22, 1947 and joined the U.S. Marine Corps as a young man. He stayed in the Marines, earning one of the highest ranks any enlisted man can earn. As a career Marine, Larry Snook has received two Purple Hearts for wounds in combat and several commendations for bravery and service to his country above and beyond the call of duty. He is a veteran of Vietnam and the Gulf War, and a graduate of Parkland College. Larry attended the University of Illinois as his grandfather C.M. Snook, Sr., his uncle Herbert, his three brothers and his father.

Q.L. recalls the day that he and Margaret met their oldest son after he had been wounded in Vietnam.

"Larry had almost been killed by a land mine explosion, and had received months of therapy and several surgeries. The day that Margaret and I went to welcome him home, I saw him heavily bandaged and being transported on a stretcher. We just cried. He hugged me and told me everything would be okay. He never complained once about the pain of those many months. It really humbled me."

Larry recovered from those wounds to return to active duty. He lives in Jacksonville, North Carolina. He had been a marine for twenty-five years. Larry supervises several newspaper distribution locations in a wide area out of Jacksonville. Larry has given Q.L. and Margaret five grandchildren: Rebecca "Becky," Christina, Angela, Amy, and Quentin Laurence III.

Q.L.'s second son, Clayton Maurice, was born on October 15, 1950, and like his father, has a heart for teaching and a mind for finance. C. Maurice Snook has earned his M.B.A. from Chapel Hill, N.C. after his bachelor's degree from the University of Illinois. He is associate dean for finance and administration for Medical University of South Carolina. Maurice is a C.P.A. He is married to wife, Jan, and they have six children: Nathan, Kelsey, Mika, John "J.C", James and Joseph.

Tom, the third child of Q.L. and Margaret, was born on March 14, 1953. He works as an inventor and businessman and resides in Savoy, Illinois. Tom developed and invented a revolutionary flashlight that can be twisted and shaped into any form so that it may be used in tight or hard-to-get-into places. The light, known as the Snook Light, is being mass produced and is in wide use. Tom is a veteran of the U.S. Army, having served in the Vietnam conflict in army security. Like his father, Tom is an airplane pilot. Tom attended Parkland, Southern Illinois University and the University of Illinois.

Sarah Louise Genevieve Snook is the only daughter of the family. She was born on April 16, 1955. Sarah and her husband, Jeff Hudson, own Hudson Agricultural Service of Charleston, Illinois, a farm management business. They have one child, Nicholas. Sarah has a B.A. from Eastern Illinois University in Charleston, Illinois. She also works in real estate sales and is a township assessor. She and her family reside near Charleston, Illinois.

The youngest of the Snook children is Earl Wesley. Born on July 14, 1957, Earl was the first member of the family to become an Eagle Scout. He lives in Mattoon, Illinois, and, following in his father's footsteps, is insurance customer service agent for Combined Insurance Company. He is an instrument commercial pilot and an experienced carpenter. Earl is a graduate of Southern Illinois University at Carbondale, after attending the University of Illinois and Parkland.

Q.L. Snook today looks and acts like a man in his mid-fifties, not in his mid-seventies. He has built a financial fortune and has had the wisdom to place that fortune in a living trust and a well-planned estate. He manages a large, diversified investment portfolio daily, is a voracious reader of newspapers, magazines and books, and still doesn't have much time to sleep. Sleep has never fit well into Q.L.'s schedule. He says that he has programmed himself to "sleep faster" so that he can fit more into every day!

Men and women half his age would have difficulty keeping up with Snook's hectic schedule. That schedule includes trips twice a month to Illinois where he has maintained a home for many years. He also has a home in Deltona, where he resides when he is not in Savoy.

Q.L. Snook has never had the need for many diversions. He is an even-tempered, yet highly driven man, an odd combination of entrepreneur and teacher. He is an intensely driven businessman, yet a man committed to helping others through a multitude of ways and causes. While he has been dictated by an intense and detailed schedule all of his life, he will drop it all just as quickly to pick a bucket of oranges for a visitor, make personal Christmas calls with gifts for his tenants and counsel a friend in need.

When the companies were in the newly remodeled offices at 202 West Hill Street, Champaign, Illinois, in June 1967, Q.L., with his wife and their four younger children, traveled three weeks in Europe. During 1966 and 1967 their oldest son, Q.L. "Larry" Junior, was on active duty with the Marines in Vietnam.

Comments

It is an honor and pleasure to comment about Mr. Snook. He was the founder and president of Thomas Jefferson Life Insurance Company in Champaign, Illinois. In 1968, I accepted a position with the company and worked there 6-1/2 years in the capacity of Director of Policy Owner Service and Assistant Secretary of the company. I found Mr. Snook to be a very fair person, a Christian, extremely civic minded and a devoted family man. It was a pleasure working with him and his company. He is a true friend.

Ruthellen Davis, Rolling Meadows, Illinois

Q.L.: Your unselfish devotion to building Thomas Jefferson Life has given the opportunity to succeed to so many and is deeply appreciated by Mozell and me.

Harlan Bliss, Bloomington, Illinois

What I remember most about Q is integrity and attitude. I dealt with Q for a number of years when he was running Thomas Jefferson Life Insurance Company and I was serving as an officer of Continental Bank of Chicago, as investment advisor to the company. Q was absolutely a "Man of his word." Secondly, Q has one of the most creative and positive ways of approaching life that I have ever encountered. His enthusiasm has built a very successful company. Q has the ability to see further and more accurately than the rest of us. That is a gift that can probably not be taught but it is a tremendous help in business and personal life. Perhaps the most important thing that Q shared with the rest of us was happiness. Q is a real joy to be with. He was always upbeat and I always felt better about myself and life in general when visiting with Q.

Daniel J. Fuss, Loomis Sayles & Company, Investment Counsel, Boston, Massachusetts

Q.L. Snook has been a vital part of my life for over thirty years. I have adopted a good portion of his philosophy of dealing with my fellow man in a very honest and straight-forward manner. Just as basic is his firm conviction that any goals you set for yourself are attainable through your own determination.

Charles R. McCarthy, Retired General Manager, The Deltona Corporation at Deltona

6

THE BUSINESS PHILOSOPHY OF Q.L. SNOOK

Seven key elements to
entrepreneurial success

Eight of ten new businesses will close in America within one year. Of the two that survive their first year, eighty percent will not see their fifth year of operation (Bureau of Labor Statistics, United States Chamber of Commerce). With odds so stacked against the small business owner, what can you do to increase your chances of being one of the few successful, enduring entrepreneurial businesses?

In his fifty years of experience, Q.L. Snook outlines seven key elements to success in starting, and successfully operating, a small business in America.

Element #1
Thoroughly examine yourself.

Do you really have it in you to risk everything you have to start a business? Do you have the work ethic to do *everything* in your business by yourself if need be? Are you willing to risk the money, knowing the odds are stacked against you? Can you afford to risk and lose it all? What about your family? Will they support you in your efforts? Can your family situation afford this type of risk? Do you have sufficient motivation to do this? What is your motivation (independence, riches, control)?

Snook maintains that every successful business begins here. You have to be a risk taker. Although you can often share the risk with hand-picked investors, you cannot be afraid of risk. You need to be more innovative than successful competitors around you. You have to work harder, longer and smarter than they do, if you stand a chance to exceed them. Snook also strongly recommends that you hand pick your investors and share work responsibilities with them, getting them involved as well.

It isn't good enough to *try it*; you'll fail if you have only a desire to *try it*. You need to focus on success, and *do it*. Trying it will only bring ruin and failure. If it is going to be, it's up to me! Be prepared to meet any opportunity.

The story of Ray Kroc, the founder of McDonald's, illustrates the point well. Kroc opened a hamburger stand and no one came. His hamburger stand was ridiculed, but he persisted. He was innovative in his speed of service and selection. He was competitive with his pricing. But even the king of the Golden Arches himself admitted that he made every mistake possible. Still he persisted. He survived, and then, finally, thrived. He risked all he had, but he *knew himself*. He believed in himself. Share the risk with investors within your marketing area. Pick investors with qualifications.

Walt Disney is another example. When Disney approached investors with the idea of making a cartoon movie, they laughed at him. No one would come. He was dreaming. Disney risked all he had. He even went bankrupt. But he *knew himself*; he knew that what he had to offer people would make them feel good. They would laugh. They would cry. Animation didn't matter. People would like it. He never doubted it. Outcast by his family for not taking the safe and secure route, Disney persisted. His empire was built because he believed in himself, even when no one else would.

Element #2:

Work for someone else in your chosen field for at least a year.

Nothing replaces experience. What better way to learn your business than to have someone else teach you, and get paid to learn it? Snook believes that to succeed in a competitive market place with a new business, that you need to know as much about that business as you possibly can. The on-the-job-training will convince you, one way or the other, whether this business is for you. "Work harder than anyone else in that company," Snook states. "Learn everything you can." After your work experience, you may conclude that this chosen field really wasn't what you wanted to do with your life in the first place!

Snook uses the example of Sam Walton, founder of Wal-Mart, as an example. Walton worked for the Ben Franklin Company for ten years before deciding to go out on his own and compete with them. He started at the bottom, as a clerk, and worked his way up, learning more and more about what he needed to do to succeed. "Patience," Snook advises, "is the key. Learn the chosen business thoroughly. Learn what your competitors are doing right, and what they are doing wrong. Then, and only then, can you compete with them."

Snook maintains that while hard work, motivation and desire are important to success, they aren't enough. "Find out what the consumer wants, then find a way to give that to them, faster, better, more economically, or with better quality, than your competitor."

Dave Thomas, the founder of Wendy's, worked for the Kentucky Fried Chicken corporation for eight years before he started Wendy's. He learned the fast-food business. He was an eager student, absorbing everything he was taught. The company loved his eagerness, and taught him more, elevating his position. Thomas learned so much working with Kentucky Fried Chicken that he was convinced he could compete with them. Only then, did he consider striking out on his own.

Element #3:
Keep your priorities clearly in focus.

Snook's business priorities are fairly simple. Everything he did in his life emphasized these priorities. Every major decision he made had these priorities firmly in focus.

- First, there are your stockholders or investors. They have entrusted you with their money and

212

you have a primary responsibility to make sure they get a return for that investment that is *more than they are now earning.* Snook was never satisfied with a good return. His work plan was designed to ensure that their investment was not only safeguarded, but also earned a higher return on their money than they are not now earning.

- Second priority was *the customer.* The customer has to be the focal point of your business. Without him/her, you have no business. Your product or service needs to be constructed and presented with the customer in mind. While this may sound like an obvious point, the truth is often the opposite. Is the customer best served by electronic answering devices? Is the customer best served when they have to wait four to six weeks for shipping? Is the customer best served when they have only one choice of color, or size? Is the customer best served if they need assistance, and you are in a meeting and can't be disturbed? Is the customer best served if you respond to them without a smile in your voice and a welcoming handshake?

Snook maintains that America has lost its competitive edge in world economics because we have lost our focus on the customer. What would appear so obvious to so many, gets so easily mired in internal policy, internal focus and internal problems. "Our focus," Snook argues, "shifted to profits, rather than customer service."

Nowhere is this more evident than in protracted labor disputes between management and unions, whether in the auto industry or in professional baseball. If our focus were the customer, and the customer was our first priority, a strike would simply never have been allowed. The point is illustrated in Japan as well. After World War II, Japanese entrepreneurs came by the thousands to America with their cameras around their necks and their notepads under their arms. They studied our products under the microscope, examining every aspect of production, service, technology, marketing, accounting, research and customer demand. Without raw materials, the Japanese bought what they needed and imported it all. Then they trained their employees that nothing else mattered beyond the customer. They brought in the raw materials, built the products, and shipped them back to America and other world markets, doing it all cheaper and with higher quality than we were doing.

Snook maintains that the auto industry lost its focus on customers and American auto makers were taken to task by the Japanese, who hadn't lost an emphasis on customers. The electronics industry lost its focus on customers and American business owners lost market share to the Japanese. The story is like a broken record, repeated again and again.

- The third priority that Snook maintains is essential to build success, is *employees*. Snook argues that successful entrepreneurs must treat their employees better than their competitors if they are to find their niche and eventually outdistance the competition; better pay, better working conditions, better employee philosophy. The old adage that a "happy employee is a productive employee," is nowhere more evident than in Japan. The Japanese built their companies with the Snook formula: Investors must prosper, customers must be paramount in all decision making, and employees must want to work for you. Japanese industrialists studied the American labor market, taking it apart inch by inch. Then they built a stronger system. They paid their employees well; they showered them with company-provided benefits unheard of in America: childcare services on site, gymnasiums for exercise, a temple for worship on site, split shifts, swing shifts, short shifts. They redefined what the employee wanted from their company, and did so by asking the employees. While America was busy dictating policy to employees, Japan was busy asking them, "What more can we do for you?" Ultimately, the American employment system had to go back to Japan to rediscover Western failings.

Stockholder security and profits, customer satisfaction and focus, employee benefits that exceed the standards; these are priorities that every successful business owner should have on top of their daily agenda, according to Snook.

Element #4:
Start with sufficient capitalization.

There are two ways to capitalize and grow your company, Snook says.

- The first is on your own, with your own money and keeping all of the ownership. While it may be a slower way to begin and grow your company, it is also a more secure way. All decisions are yours to make; all gain, and, conversely, all risk, is also yours to take.

The amount of capital needed depends on the type of product or service you will be performing. Having done your homework, you should know from experience how long it will take to generate sufficient income to begin posting profits. With 1,200,000 bankruptcies in America last year, four times more than the previous year, Snook is adamant about the need for adequate funding, however.

"Most small businesses start with too little capital. It is one of the primary causes of business failure within the first three years," Snook maintains. Snook also states that once you've created a business plan and have a pretty good idea of how much capital it will take before you start making a profit, the "amount you projected should be doubled." It is too easy to be too positive about early projections, unless they are based upon excellent market studies.

Snook believes firmly that to succeed in a sole proprietorship, or small one-person corporation, it is essential *not to borrow the start-up capital*. First, it is a bad way to start a business. Remember that experience, desire and hard work are not the only factors involved in succeeding in your business. Going into debt to start your company is not recommended. If you don't have the money to start the company, you should probably postpone the venture.

Once the business is begun and contracts are being written, Snook suggests that if borrowing is necessary, borrow for "working capital." Working capital is the money needed to fulfill sales demand. When new business owners are able to produce contracts and work orders, banks are more likely to loan them money so that these orders can be fulfilled and profits made.

One final word on borrowing money, according to Snook: Long-term debt for purposes of buying a building, purchasing needed equipment to streamline the operation, etc., is good debt. It is the type of debt necessary to generate profit, and it is debt that can be backed up by assets, rather than to take cash to purchase your office or equipment.

No matter how your company is funded and how it obtains working capital, Snook strongly recommends that you need to maintain good financial, sales and company records. "Every business needs to employ a good lawyer, a banker and an accountant."

- The *second* way to capitalize your business is to *form a corporation of investors and stockholders* and raise the money needed to form the business, create working capital and make needed purchases of land, equipment and technology up-front.

Snook masterfully created the Holding Corporation of America and Thomas Jefferson Life in this fashion.

To sell others on your plan, it is vital that you have a good plan, says Snook. The plan needs to be as professionally designed as possible, since you'll be asking others to invest their savings in your idea. Snook advises that in order to raise money to advance your plan, you need to have a strong and demonstrated success pattern behind you, and that you must also invest money in your own project. "That makes the investor more secure, knowing you're also putting in money, as well as your experience."

Snook maintains that it is helpful to be well-known in the community and involved in many community activities. "Your character and experience are what people will be investing in," Snook says. "Your goals must be attainable and honorable. Your methods must be above reproach. "

Another approach if you are already in business and wish to further capitalize, is to go to your suppliers who do business with you and let them know of an opportunity to invest in your firm.

Whether you have decided to attract a few investors or many, they must be kept informed from the start, advises Snook. In the formative stages of your company, the investors must be aware of your progress.

It is for this very reason, that Snook explains that the good investor is more than someone who simply invests money. The good investor should add far more. Perhaps they have an experience area, such as accounting, finance, legal, or sales that they can add to. They should be asked and expected to advance the promotion and sales of the company as much as they are able, in their own geographic area and their own sphere of influence. In some cases, they may become your first clients, and maybe even your best clients.

Snook advanced his idea for the Holding Corporation of America by seeking investors who could not only afford to invest (and possibly even lose their investment), but also who would be important to advance the sales plan for the new life insurance company in their own cities. Most of Snook's investors became his first sales of insurance. Some of them joined his management team and his advisory board.

"The good investor is not a static investor," Snook says. "The person must be able to afford to lose their entire investment. They must also be able to qualify for service to the company. If those two criteria can't be met, then it is far better to reject them when you begin, rather than face an unhappy and unproductive investor after you are established."

When forming a corporation made up of investors and stockholders, it is important that the board of directors is selected carefully and wisely. Snook maintains that the board should not be made up of your closest business advisors, such as your lawyer, your accountant or perhaps your banker. While these members of your team are important, they probably will not serve the company and the goals of the company well as board members, in Snook's experience.

"Your closest friends can turn against you," Snook argues. It happened in his own company. When properly funded and ready to expand and grow, some of his closest advisors and friends were at odds with him.

How much capital is enough to form your company? Snook will smile if asked this question and usually reply wryly, "You can never have too much money. Whether you go it alone or with a group of investors, raise all the money you can, being as liberal with your projections and as pessimistic about the first few months as you can."

Element #5:
Hire the best staff available.

Snook's business philosophy is fairly basic and simple:

Always treat your stockholders with profits.

Always treat your customer with the best product and service you can provide, which should be something they cannot get elsewhere.

Always treat your employees with respect, good working conditions and excellent pay and benefits.

Show them how they can earn more, by giving more of themselves. Let them become important to your business goals and philosophy and most employees will respond. Simple business philosophy, but also a rare one in today's business world. In Snook's opinion, it isn't just about being "a nice guy." Treating your employees right makes good business sense.

"When Sam Walton created Wal-Mart, he made sure that his employees were called "associates," rather than given a number. He made sure they were kept informed, kept motivated through company picnics, events and functions. He made sure they were paid just a little better than they were being paid by Wal-Mart's competitors. He made sure that the benefits the company offered were better than anyone else's in the area. It is not surprising that he drew some of the best employees from every community where he started a store."

It is wise your management team treats employees better than your competition. Again, Q.L. Snook:

"When we were looking to fill top management positions, we spared no expense to find the right individual. Often I would employ recruitment firms to help me find the right person for the job. I paid them better than they could make anywhere else. After all, the company was going to offer a better service than anyone else could offer, so I knew I needed a better individual to fill top jobs; however, they must show them how to earn their pay."

Although paying your employees well is vital to a healthy and prospering business, research shows that employee pay isn't always the top concern of American workers. Working conditions, company benefits, job flexibility, advancement opportunity and company philosophy are major considerations for most workers. When structuring your employee benefit program, Snook advises that you regularly converse with your employees. Involve them in the decision-making process of the company; encourage their opinions and suggestions.

Snook uses the Japanese worker as an example of why this philosophy is effective:

"When the workforce in the United States was striking against the ownership of the company, the Japanese were building gymnasiums for their employees, providing day care facilities, flexible work schedules and improving company morale to beat us in the global economy. While we alienated our workers, they endeared their workers to their employers. It showed in their quality products and services. Now America has to play catch up."

Element #6:
Know how to find sales.

Every company needs sales, but start-up companies need sales the most. You have a good idea, you've done your homework and researched the product, the competition, pricing, etc.; perhaps you've even hired some good help to aid you; but now, you need sales.

One of Q.L. Snook's talents throughout his career has been the ability to find prospects. He has always known that he had quality products to promote. He also knew that once he could find a qualified prospect, he had an excellent chance of selling them. But where to find the prospects?

When Snook's father, Clayton, began the portable feed mill during the Depression, Snook witnessed how a young company could grow if you treated your customers well.

"My dad took such good care of his customers that the word spread. People appreciated the convenience, the personal service. They started telling their neighbors, and when their neighbors were satisfied, they told their neighbors, and my dad's business grew and grew."

From that experience, Snook expanded on the basic idea. Good service wasn't enough. Most people might not think to refer you, even if they like your product and service. Snook developed a referral system which not only worked, but was copied and used by organizations large and small, and is still in use today. While the system itself was unique to Snook, he modified it, organized it, and sold it. The results were staggering.

From his roots in the construction business in the 1950s, through his early years in insurance, and then, teaching his own agents with companies such as Land Of Lincoln, Republic Investors Life and Thomas Jefferson Life, as well as the founding and organization of the Holding Corporation of America, Snook fashioned a unique referral plan that set him apart from his competition. His referral system was so well-defined and orchestrated, that international companies like the Deltona Corporation and the Mackle brothers used it.

Snook built a career around this simple, yet seldom-used system of referral. He rarely advertised; he never needed to. Usually, he had all the prospects he could handle. When the five names lead to five more names, the pyramid of potential prospects, all qualified and referred, totals twenty-five names. In time, you have all the prospects you could possibly call on. Snook spoke confidently about the referral system, because he knew it worked. It had built his construction business, his real estate business, his insurance business, his investment business. It had built the formation of stock sales for the Holding Corporation of America, raising $4,000,000 in one year, overselling the stock issue.

Snook's referral system built stock sales and insurance sales for Thomas Jefferson Life, a new insurance firm in a competitive market, and caused the company to become one of the most recognized and respected insurance firms in Illinois. Snook believed in the system and taught it to all of his agents. They rehearsed it, practiced it, role played with objections and, inevitably, learned it and succeeded with it.

Snook's summary of a good sales call is as follows:

1) Always answer a question with a question. He had learned that one many years ago from his dad.

2) When you think you have exhausted everything, simply ask, "Why?" Being persistent and being ready for objections is the key to successful selling and closing.

3) Never ask a customer to "sign." Always ask him to write his name on the necessary information sheet. Signing can be threatening and permanent. Your choice of words needs to be reassuring.

4) Use the phrase, "Don't you agree?" frequently. By receiving affirmation, you are overcoming objections.

5) Always have husband and wife together for a presentation requiring a large amount of money from them. Without knowing who handled the money and financial decisions, it was important to have both parties present, so one wouldn't have to hesitate or wait to talk with the other. They could discuss the matter right then.

6) Remember, everyone wants your product, and probably needs your product to enhance their life. You

believe in your product; so sell them your dream, making it theirs as well.

Element #7:

Start your company as though it will be yours forever.

Key to any business success is a detailed, well thought out business plan. When properly executed and adjustments made along the way, Snook advises that most young businesses would survive the critical first or second year.

Snook also advises that you can't go into business and say, "Well, I'll give it a try." He strongly maintains that *trying* just isn't good enough.

"Start your business as though it's going to last forever, and that you intend to run it forever," Snook says. Like the home builder that he has been all of his life, Snook likens starting a business to building a home.

"Capital, character and capacity," Snook is fond of saying, "are the building blocks of a good business. It all begins with a strong foundation, strong walls, insulated windows, good roof and some comfort inside at an affordable price."

In addition to the seven elements required for success, you should also be aware that:

1. All progress in society and business has been made because of *dissatisfaction*. Both positive and

negative, we move forward or backward because the true entrepreneur is constantly *dissatisfied*.

2. There is *always* a price for success: *always*.

3. You should *never* give up.

4. Those closest to you will try to *manipulate* you through a variety of means. Your closest, inner circle may not always have your, and your company's, best interests at heart. Be on guard against *manipulation*.

Building blocks for success

1. Fund your company properly, either on your own or with a group of investors.

2. Start your business as though you intend it to last forever.

3. Find the needs and wants of the market, and fill them.

4. Find a niche in the market that no one else, or few others, might have.

5. Honesty and integrity are vital to your success. Do not compromise your principles, no matter what.

6. Service and quality, service and quality— memorize these two words and repeat them every day.

7. Quit dreaming and get started.

8. Don't be afraid to start small. Be conservative. Learn and adjust your plan as you go. Flexibility is the key.

9. Use the referral system described in this book to find all the sales prospects necessary to

succeed. Keep traditional advertising costs affordable.

10. Hire the best people you can find. Treat them better than they are used to being treated. Listen to them; learn from them.

11. Run your business profitably. Do not be afraid of making profit. Profits fuel your growth and guarantee your survival.

12. Be prepared for the worst of conditions.

13. Your customer must need you always—you must help him grow, improve his life, and be a constant benefit to him.

14. Be happy with your work. When work becomes fun, you have already succeeded. Not only love what you do, but *be in love* with what you do.

15. Invest your profits wisely.

16. Borrow conservatively and only for the right reasons.

17. See your company as global in scope, even

though right now you may serve only a local neighborhood. Plan big. Dream big. Be bold and decisive, even if you make mistakes.

18. Accept mistakes as normal operating procedure. The key is to learn from mistakes.

19. You should always be looking to improve, offer better service, offer more services, be ready to move quickly.

20. Keep good records. An accountant, a banker and a lawyer are keys to your successful future. They don't necessarily need to manage your company.

21. Serve your community and fellow man. Give back what has been given to you, and more rewards will surely come your way. Make a commitment or a promise to this end.

Q.L. Snook is a self-made man. He is admired by people throughout the country. People everywhere have been impressed by his drive, his intensity, his passion for business and his tenacity for squeezing as much time into every day of his life. He has profited by his efforts, but he has done so without compromising his principles and his underlying belief that man is good, and our future is bright.

Anyone who knows Quentin Laurence Snook knows that he has never been afraid to take the road less traveled. He has lived true to himself, to his family and to his Creator, and has touched so many lives in a positive way.

His manner is giving and open. He is always teaching: sharing his philosophy, his energy, his belief that goodness can happen, if we only believe it will.

He thanks God for his life of blessings. He also thanks his family and friends.

Comments

Q.L. Snook has been my friend since 1961. At that time he explained an impressive plan of his while in my kitchen. He is a very enthusiastic, dynamic and convincing person. He has retained those traits to this day. In 1978 I asked Q.L. to become involved in the Boy Scouts. As busy as he was, he enthusiastically said yes. He quickly rose to become Council President and later was Chairman of the Board of Trustees and Sustaining Membership Director for raising funds. His efforts were instrumental in purchasing a large addition to the Council Scout Camp. In 1971 Q.L. initiated a group that became known as "Stairway to the Stars" of the First United Methodist Church in Champaign. He gave sizeable gifts to the building projects and operations of our church over the years. He and Mrs. Snook have been pillars of our community. He has done so many, many good things that it would be impossible for me to list them. I am proud to call him my friend.

Wayne Weber, Champaign, Ill.

If I had to put my relationship with Q.L. Snook in a capsule, I would say that Q.L. could write a book on the power of positive thinking. I believe another gentleman was famous for doing this, but Q.L. had the same philosophy and practiced it always. I had the pleasure of serving on a museum board with Mr. Snook. His advice and counsel were so important in getting the museum off the ground. His work with Kiwanis has been outstanding. I wish I could be as faithful and loyal a member as Q.L. He has more than 45 years of perfect attendance and is a true leader in the club. That's what life is all about...loyalty, *leadership, and responsibility to one's fellow man. Q.L. is also blessed with a loving and caring wife. Margaret is a very special and very helpful person.*

Louis D. Liay, Executive Director,
University of Illinois Alumni Assn., Urbana, IL

We probably cannot thank you both enough for all your generosity during the past several months. For that matter, there is really no way to thank you for all the diaper changes, trips to the doctor, saxophone lessons, travel to camp outs, words of encouragement and advice, etc., etc. With each passing year, it becomes ever clearer that parenting is a lifelong career. I hope that you can be proud of most of what we do. I am thankful for what I have—both sets of children, a number of material things, for being married to Jan and for having you as parents.

Maurice Snook, Son, Charleston, South Carolina

For years I have considered myself as one with a more than adequate vocabulary, but when it comes to expressing my feelings about you, I am at a true loss for words. Thank you seems so small, and yet, my heart is filled with joy—not just because my news was so good, but that you, two of the busiest people in our area, took the time and effort to take me to such a wonderful doctor! I am still almost slap-happy with gladness—what a super wonderful thing for you two to do for anyone, let alone me. I will never be able to thank you for your many kindnesses. You are both so special and will forever be in my heart, while I am forever in your debt. You are both such remarkable people. Your lives have

233

been filled with great challenges each of which it is obvious, you have handled to the very hilt of satisfaction. You both have given so much, not just to your own family, but to so many in so many places. Your efforts in Deltona alone, have been so much admired and utilized by so many in helping their lives to be richer.
Beverly Stuhrenberg-Tracchio, Deltona, Florida

My relationship with Quentin came about when he did a fine job building my first house. His work ethic and civic leadership, particularly with MATTHEW HOUSE (a home for distressed children), have been widely recognized.
Lee P. Eilbracht,
Retired Executive Director of American
Baseball Coaches Assn., Champaign, Illinois

I became acquainted with Q.L. Snook while I served as pastor of the First United Methodist Church of Deltona, Florida, from 1975 to 1981. During the months that he was here, he lent his support financially, mentally and physically to the growth of the church. Q.L. Snook is an honest, decent man, and his lifestyle is impeccable.
Rev. Lee Davidson, Retired,
Orange City, Florida

I am proud to regard Q.L. Snook as a close friend. We first met in 1982, shortly after I joined the local Kiwanis club where he has been a member almost fifty years. I had just taken early retirement from the faculty of Southern Illinois University at Carbondale and was beginning to

234

circulate more in the community. Q.L. helped me to find some new opportunities. Q.L. invited me to join a local SCORE (Senior Corps of Retired Executives) chapter that he belonged to. This is one place he demonstrated his willingness and ability to help others to succeed. He has had personal experience with a wide variety of businesses, plus helping others to plan and better manage their own businesses. My friend is an entrepreneur from broad experience in many business, charity and community affairs, and is quite willing to share what he had learned with all who wish to know.

James A. Robb,
Retired College Professor, Savoy, Illinois

One of my greatest childhood experiences happened in kindergarten being picked up at noon by my dad and then sitting on his lap flying his airplane to Grandma's house for lunch. This happened more than once. No one can work as hard as my dad. I've been with him digging deep ditches for drainage, and he works non-stop. He has taught me to have a positive attitude. Thanks, Dad.

Thomas Snook, Son, Savoy, Illinois

Q.L. and Marge have been precious friends of mine for many, many years. My former husband, Oscar C. Plumb, was the minister of the First United Methodist Church of Champaign, Illinois. He died many years ago. Q. L. Snook was a very important person in our church, as I am sure he has been during the past years as well. Q.L. is great!

Helen Elkin, Lakeland, Florida

It is easy to comment on Q.L....even favorably. I have known him through most of my adult life. I have seen him advise SCORE clients. I have observed him as a successful entrepreneur. But most of all, when I think of Q.L., I think of his multiple contributions to causes. He is a benefactor par excellence. Much of this he does quietly and with no desire for recognition. How much better this world would be with more Q.L.s!

Byron Vedder, SCORE Volunteer,
Champaign, Illinois

Q.L. Snook was born in Normal, Illinois, in 1922. He became a member of the Bloomington Lodge No. 43, Bloomington, Illinois, in June of 1945 transferring his membership to Western Star Lodge No. 240 in April 1975. He became a Life Member in 1993 and a 50-year member in 1995. We are proud of Mr. Snook and are appreciative of his efforts in our Lodge.

Rob Beldon, Secretary,
Western Star Lodge #240, Champaign, Illinois

For the purpose of my father's biography, and for his purpose of sharing his experiences that may be useful to others trying to build wealth and success, I would like to provide some examples of his influence on my life.

I recall my first job, at about eight years old. I was making homemade cookies and Kool-aid to tote around the neighborhood in my red wagon. My hope was to sell to the home builders and workers. I don't remember selling many cookies and Kool-aid, or earning anything from it. But making money wasn't the essence of the matter. It was more of an accomplishment to feel helpful in providing a service and being accepted within the realm of adults. This was my entry into the business world.

My father was in the home construction business. All of the homes we lived in while growing up were in new subdivisions and were built by my father. I helped my father in some way or another at various building sites from my earliest memory, probably from age five until my junior year in high school. We probably moved a dozen times in as many years.

I was introduced to a variety of hard working men who worked with my father. Some of them were displaced persons from Hungary. I saw and learned from the interactions between these men and the working relationship between them and my father. These were my first adult role models.

Briefly, I will list a few other projects that helped instill entrepreneurial skills and better prepared me to rely upon myself very early as an adolescent.

I helped out after school at my father's real estate and insurance office, Q.L. Snook Enterprises. I emptied the trash, vacuumed, and did other tasks for Mrs. Witt, my father's secretary.

I sold popcorn for a couple of years that we grew in our garden. We always had a vegetable garden.

We had a Welsh pony that I gave neighborhood kids rides on. I charged twenty-five cents, sometimes less.

When we lived next to the U. of Illinois golf course I sold golf balls that I found. One summer we had a miniature golf course built for the kids in the neighborhood.

I also ran a trap line for three years selling the muskrat and racoon hides. Corn detasseling was my first real job where I worked for someone else and earned a wage. I did this for two summers when I was thirteen and fourteen.

I also worked at Camp Miniwanca in Michigan for a few weeks the summer before finishing high school.

These first work experiences reinforced the discipline and sense of responsibility that had already been instilled within me by my father.

I was very active in 4-H, Boy Scouts, and the church, while growing up.

My father always stressed the importance of presenting myself in a professional, respectful manner. I learned to be patient, to be on time, and to provide a service with a smile. I was encouraged to work within my means and resources. I developed self-reliance and confidence from initiatives encouraged by my parents.

The idea of working for somebody else was not encouraged. Finding ways to become independent was always emphasized. The free enterprise system was believed in strongly and my father was proof that it works.

I served 25 years in the Marine Corps and since retirement in 1993, have been self-employed in the same line of work delivering newspapers and magazines. I was sole proprietor of a small retail business for one year, and have worked as a life insurance agent.

My own tradition of serving myself while serving others through self-employment is a direct result of my father's example. It has always been another tradition for me to give something back to the community through volunteer service. I have followed my father's example, being a Red Cross volunteer and a member of REACT International, helping with USO and United Way projects as well as Boy and Girl Scouting. I also served as a volunteer with N.C. National Guard for five years. All these volunteer activities have been since leaving the Marine Corps.

Quentin Laurence Snook, Jr., Son
Jacksonville, North Carolina

Although I had heard of Mr. Snook and his "community conscience" often since moving to the Champaign area in 1968, my first personal contact was in a business situation in 1984. Q.L. has always been easy to work with and a very good businessman. His knowledge of investments and business in general is extensive. He is always willing and anxious to share his expertise.

Outside of the business arena, I know Mr. Snook through our local Kiwanis Club. Q.L. has been an active member with perfect attendance since 1948. His dedication to and belief in Kiwanis is to be modeled. I had the privilege of being sponsored by Q.L. as one of the early female members of the Champaign-Urbana, Illinois Kiwanis Club.

Thank you for your invitation to comment on my relationship with Q.L. Snook.

Rhea A. Lawrence, CFP/CTFA
Vice President, Bank Illinois Trust Company
Champaign, Illinois

It gives me great pleasure to tell you that I have known Quentin L. Snook for almost fifty years as a builder, administrator and philanthropist. He has been a contractor, real estate salesman, founder of the Thomas Jefferson Life Insurance Company, fifty year member of the Champaign-Urbana Kiwanis Club (tenth largest in the world), and a dynamic friend who was an enthusiastic promoter of his business adventures and later for quiet philanthropic interests.

He was always ready to support youth programs, community improvement projects, and social well-being projects. I have known him through generous donations to the Methodist Church and so many other organizations.

He was an enthusiastic presenter to stimulate additional support of projects in many charitable activities. He and his wife are friendly and modest people who truly enjoy living in America. I wish success for his book and look forward to receiving a copy.

Glenn E. Stout, President
International Water Resources Assn.
University of Illinois, Urbana, Illinois

240

As Downstate Illinois Chairman of the National Council on Crime and Delinquency (NCCD), one of my tasks was to promote a good police image and work closely with police chiefs in an effort to resolve problems involving racial tension, along with antagonism toward the police through our Public Friend Number One program.... It looked like we were not going to get the project off the ground, until I talked to Bob Pope and Quentin Snook. The two of them gave us enough support to proceed.

The billboard campaign idea was picked up by the national office of the NCCD and they gave us publicity, and I was told that the idea was used many places around the country. It would have died on the vine had it not been for the generosity of Mr. Pope and Mr. Snook.

Homer H. Bash, Champaign, Illinois

Mr. Snook, or Q.L., is quite an amazing person. I first met him when I moved to Deltona, Florida taking the position as the first career Fire Chief of this new community. I knew that Q.L. had been instrumental in developing Deltona and helping to shape it over the years.

Q.L. rented a home to me in 1984, when I first arrived. He has been a part of our family for over 13 years.

When you first meet Q.L. you might not realize just how successful he is. He might spend half of your time talking to your children, reciting to them the alphabet, backwards, or presenting them a gift. For my son James, those gifts have been many: interesting books, toys, his first Scout knife, a metal pocket perpetual calendar. Just try to leave without some oranges or grapefruit grown in his

241

backyard! I have heard him tell my son on several occasions that he could do whatever he wanted to do, if he tried. In fact, I wonder if he was talking to me on several of those occasions.

Q.L.'s belief in the future of our children shows in his interest and time given to such organizations as the Boys and Girls Club of Deltona, and the YMCA. If he can't be there, a donation will be. During my conversations with him, I have heard of his love for God and his belief that God has given him all the worldly goods that he and Margaret enjoy.

Margaret shares the experience of Q.L. on a 24-hour basis. She is an extension of Q.L.'s happiness with the world and our community.

Q.L. is a businessman; shoulder to the wheel, nose to the grindstone, type of man. But he is never too busy to help out someone in need.

He has been there for me as a mentor in my goal for a safe, protected community. He, too, has helped me establish my own business and gives me advice regularly.

Q.L. has been instrumental in helping win our incorporation as a community. He has helped educate our residents, politicians and business people about the many benefits that this government could bring. He speaks from experience.

Q.L. has always been there for me. When I was under attack about my position on incorporation, Q.L. was beside me, personally and financially. He literally risked his position in the community to stand up for me, and I'll never forget that. The community has benefitted from Q.L.

Snook. I have as well, as so will you if you ever have the opportunity to meet him.

Mike Holland, Fire Chief, Deltona, Florida

As I had the opportunity to grow up with my family, it was a great experience to love and share in the inspirational moments with my father.

With his business ventures we had lots of opportunities to travel. We went once halfway around the world when I was nine years old. Many times we were in Florida. At Alligator Creek we saw gators "running" free.

Our family saw the New York's World Fair in 1964 when Father flew us over the Statue of Liberty on our approach to LaGuardia Airport in our Cessna.

My father is one of the most positive persons that I have personally known. Positive Mental Attitude all the way. For him, no obstacle is too difficult to overcome.

Earl Wesley Snook, Son, Mattoon, Illinois

Thanks for being my dad. At each step of my life, you have been with me. You have taken my hand, spoken words of praise, provided a listening ear and, at times, given correction with love.

As I get older, I can see that being a parent is not an easy job. I'll never forget the time I drove the car into the garage. Mom said that I had to call you at the office and tell you what happened. Well, if I remember correctly, my driving privileges were revoked until further notice. The next morning, before I had gotten up, you came to my bedroom to talk about "the incident." You sat on my bed

243

and we went over everything that happened. You told me that you knew it was an accident. Already, you had begun to repair the damage to the garage. This wasn't the end of my driving career, and my driving privileges were reinstated. You handed the car key back to me. We hugged, and I know I was crying. You let me know that not all things could be "fixed", but the garage was something that could be fixed. You showed me your love for me.

You gave your time to encourage me, never complaining about making sacrifices that you made to give to your family. How you managed all of your accomplishments, it is hard for me to imagine. Mom had to fill in quite often when you were out of town on business, but you were there when we needed you. Words can never express how much love I have for you and my appreciation for all that you have done for me....

Sarah Snook Hudson, Daughter, Charleston, Illinois

I met Q.L. in his earlier years at Illinois Wesleyan University in Bloomington, Illinois. I will never forget that day. I was in the library to do research work and I sat down at a table close to him. He possessed a winning smile, and an interest in me. We became good friends. I soon saw that he was a great person. I discovered that he had relentless energy, singleness of purpose, and a great ambition.

World War II developed and we each did our duty to promote the interest of our country. We each moved to Champaign, Illinois. Neither of us knew the other was there. He was teaching economics at a community college, and I had entered at law school at the University of Illinois. I had a job teaching Econ 10, as an assistant. We eventually found that we were both living in the same city.

Our meetings were many. We knew that our world was vast, that human knowledge was not manageable, that every science was growing into many more. That governments were bringing all kinds of new social programs into focus, and that change was causing many secure persons to become insecure. We knew that we had to be successful and could only be if our concept of the economic horizon proved to be correct. We had to blend these with quality in courage, energy, honesty, and singleness of purpose. We knew that if our actions were to be of importance that the service we rendered had to be of equal value to our pay. Our services would then survive in a changing world. It was our intent to bring positive results. We have each done that since that day.

We each built our own homes, with our own hands. We gained an essence of joy - living in a house, self-made. Quentin went on to become a qualified builder in both Illinois and Florida. He was able to quickly perceive the relevant truths. He learned real estate law. This factor, along with his knowledge of lots and homes, gave him the ability to represent the Mackle Brothers land transactions in Florida in a very effective way. He made a lot of money for many people.

This success did not satisfy his inward self. The joy he searched for was in something much bigger and more complicated. He had talked to me many times about creating a life insurance company in Illinois. He wanted to create one with the most capital of any that had started. He did this. He selected bright people and $8 million of stock was sold in the life company and its associated holding company. There were many stockholders that made up the original client base. This company could have become a great company because Quentin was capable in all respects. He sold his stock a few years later, and had no function in the company. The company later fell into hands of those who put it into bankruptcy.

A person who had success all of his life can have only repugnance for what took place. Failure in most things cannot be accepted in a progressive society. There is a sea of knowledge available for anyone charting the path of a company or running a speed boat.

Q.L. has been very active during most of his business life in raising money for charitable organizations. He is able to discover the real function of the organization and to create the desire and spirit to refinance. He has never made a charge for this service.

Knowledge of this man would not be complete without learning of his success in buying houses and other types of living facilities. He has many of them. He manages the operation in both Florida and Illinois.

He is a gentle man with a keen mind, and he has a high sense of responsibility. His loving wife Margaret, the pride and joy of his life, is always informed of his activities. They are both my personal friends. Our world has great need of more people like them.

Rodger Bliss, Towanda, Illinois

A Brief Chronology of
Personal and Professional Milestones

1929	Starting work with father, C.M. Snook at the Snook Feed Mill, Bloomington, IL.
1940-1942	Attended Illinois Wesleyan University
1943-1944	Served in the U.S. Navy
1942	Aircraft Owners & Pilots Assn. member, commercial pilot
1945	Joined Western Star Masons Lodge,#240, Champaign, IL.
1945	Served in the U.S. Army
1947	B.S. from the University of Illinois
1947	Founder Q.L. Snook Construction Co.
1947-1962	Agent, Kansas City Life
1947	Founder Q.L. Snook Agency
1947	Business Instructor, Ill. Comm. College
Since 1948	Member, Champaign-Urbana Noon Kiwanis Club; Legion of Honor. 1979-1980 Kiwanian of the Year Award. 1982-1983 President.
1962	Vice president, Land of Lincoln Life
1962	President/Investor/Promoter, Parkhill Manor, Punta Gorda, FL.
1962	Agent, General Development Corp.
1962	Regional Supervisor, Republic Investors
1963	Founder Q.L. Snook Securities Company

1963-1974	Founder Florida-Illinois Realty; Franchise dealer for Deltona Corp.
1964-1974	Founder, Chairman of the Board, President, Holding Corp. of America
1965-1974	Founder, Chairman of the Board, President, Thomas Jefferson Life Insurance Company of America
1965	Honored as Kentucky Colonel
1967	Chairman of the Board, President, Western Life Insurance Company
1971	Member, Newcomen Society of America
1972-1974	Founder, Chairman of the Board, Thomas Jefferson Indemnity Ins. Co.
1972	"Boss of the Year," Natl. Secr. Assn.
1974	Financial Consultant, Builder and Manager of Florida and Illinois Real Estate Properties
1974	Life Member, Univ. Illinois Alumni
1975	Champaign Historical Museum Trustee
1976-1980	McKinley YMCA Trustee, Pres. 1976-77
1976	Arrowhead Council, BSA, President
1977	Lay Speaker, First United Methodist
1977	Girls Club of America Board, Champaign, Illinois
1982	Received Silver Beaver Award, BSA
1983	University YMCA Trustee
1983	Univ. Of Illinois Adv. Board of YMCA
1983	Developmental Services Center, Business Advisory Board
1983-1993	SCORE Advisory Council, President
1970-1995	University of Illinois lecturer, MBA Business Instructor, Parkland College

Photo
Album

Genevieve and Clayton M. Snook, Sr., 1940

Clayton Morris Snook, Jr., Wilbur, Shirley, Q.L., Sr., Ruth Marian, Esther and Herbert Franklin Snook. About 1936 in front of the Ford truck with the portable grinder mounted on the flat bed, the portable feed mill.

Front: Q.L., Sr., Ruth Marian, Esther, Herbert. Back: Wilbur, Shirley, Mother, Father and Morris. 1938.

Homestead at 2405 S. Main, Rt. 51 South, Bloomington, Ill. The original feed mill building is behind the house on the right.

37th wedding anniversary for Mr. & Mrs. C.M. Snook. Front: Genevieve holding Q.L. Snook, Jr., Clayton, Marlene, Esther Kinzinger Snook, Joan, Wilbur, Paul Smith, husband of Ruth Marian with children David and Barbara. Back: Hartwell Howard, Q.L. with Clayton Maurice, Shirley, Vernon Hintborn with son Richard, Ruth Marian, Margaret. Photo by Herbert Snook, not pictured.

Original Snook's Feed Mill, 2405 S. Main, Bloomington.

The new mill was dedicated on April 24, 1948 the 34th anniversary of owners Mr. and Mrs. C.M. Snook, Senior.

Q.L. graduating from the University of Illinois, June 1947

Houghton school, Bloomington, Ill.

Hartwell Carver Howard, Jr., cousin to Q.L., 1945.

Q.L. in Ft. Knox, Kentucky, 1945, U.S. Army.

Q.L. as a V-5 Naval Cadet, 1944.

Q.L. and Margaret. May 14, 1945, engagement day.

Q.L. and Margaret, July 21, 1946, wedding day.

First home, 307 Ells Avenue, Champaign, Ill.

June 1947, B.S. from University of Illinois.

Bloomington High School graduation, 1940.

1955, a Q.L. Snook home built for his family.

FLYING OFFICE. Q.L. Snook of Q.L. Snook Enterprises,
206 W. Springfield Ave., C., is seen beside the new six
passenger Cessna 205 he recently purchased for use in his
Deltona, FL, real estate interests. He found a plane
necessary for transporting people to and from Deltona who
are interested in purchasing property for retirement and
investment. A full time pilot will be employed to fly
interested parties to Deltona on a personalized basis.

Q.L. Snook and Mrs. Nora Witt, 1967.

Million-Dollar Policy. Quentin L. Snook, center, president of Holding Corporation of America, Champaign, examines the $1,000,000 insurance policy recently purchased on his life through Kentucky Central Life Insurance Company, of Lexington, KY. Looking on at Lexington are Garvice D. Kincaid, left, Kentucky Central president, and John D. Willis, general agent for the insurer in Champaign, who sold the insurance. The policy, written as "key man" insurance, lists Snook's company as the beneficiary.

Land of Lincoln, 1962, Vice President, Q.L. Snook.

Q.L. Snook addressing HCA & TJL stockholders, 1966.

Paris, France with family, June 1966.

Land of Lincoln Life. Ray Powell, Art Thomas, Q.L., Bill Horsley, officers of the company.

1967 dedication of the newly remodeled open house and home offices of TJL and HCA at 202 W. Hill in Champaign, Ill. Mayor Virgil Wikoff cuts ribbon. Front row: Genevieve, Margaret and Q.L.

FORMING A GIANT LIFE
INSURANCE COMPANY

1965, Q.L. Snook founder

WESTERN LIFE

INSURANCE COMPANY OF AMERICA

SERVICE WITH INTEGRITY SINCE 1894

7701 CLAYTON ROAD

ST. LOUIS, MISSOURI 63117

Western Life Insurance Company of St. Louis was purchased by Thomas Jefferson Life Insurance Co. Of America

CHOSEN TOP BOSS. Quentin L. Snook, president of Thomas Jefferson Life Insurance Company of America, accepts a plaque bearing his name for being selected the 1972 Boss of the Year by the Champaign-Urbana Chapter of the National Secretaries Association. With him are Mrs. Janis Neal, left, his secretary, who submitted an essay explaining what made him an ideal boss to a panel of judges, and Mrs. Dwain Collins, one of the co-chairmen. The 17th Annual Boss Night was held in the Ramada Inn with 50 members and their bosses in attendance. Mrs. Donna Matteson, mistress of ceremonies, and Arthur Carroll, director, Governor's Office of Science and Technology, 1971 Boss of the Year, presented the award. Mrs. Jon Majors served as the other co-chairman with the assistance of Mrs. Michael Shannon.

Robert Mackle, Q.L. Snook, Frank Mackle, Jr., Elliott Mackle, 1964. Officers of the Deltona Corporation with Florida-Illinois Realty Representative, Q.L. Snook.

Q.L. Snook giving key note address to a Mackle Brothers Sales convention, 1964.

Parkhill Manor is a Florida home park that Q.L. helped develop and promote, 1962.

202 W. Hill St., Champaign, Ill. HCA & TJL home office.

Opening of Girls Club, Champaign, 1978, one of many activities promoted by Q.L. with the Kiwanis Club Committee members.

Son Larry (Q.L., Jr.) with children Angela, Amy and father, Q.L., 1980.

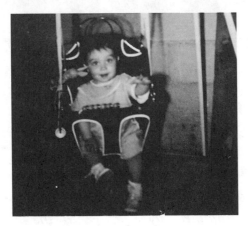

Maurice, 1951. One year old.

The Snook family, 1966, Savoy, Ill. Front: Sarah Louise, Margaret, Earl Wesley. Back: Thomas Lee, Q.L. Sr., Q.L., "Larry," Jr., Clayton Maurice.

1990 family reunion, Savoy, Ill. Margaret, Q.L., Earl, Nathan, son of C.M. Snook, Sarah, Kelsey, daughter of C.M. Snook, Clayton Maurice, Nicholas, son of Sarah, Mika, daughter of C.M., Thomas. Larry was in the Marines.

C. Maurice Snook family

Son Earl at graduation from Southern Illinois University in Carbondale, Ill., 1981.

Daughter Sarah at graduation from Eastern Illinois University in Charleston, Ill., 1979.

The Objects of
Kiwanis International

To give primacy to the human and spiritual, rather than to the material values of life.

To encourage the daily living of the Golden Rule in all human relationships.

To promote the adoption and the application of higher social, business, and professional standards.

To develop, by precept and example, a more intelligent, aggressive, and serviceable citizenship.

To provide through Kiwanis Clubs, a practical means to form enduring friendships, to render altruistic service, and to build better communities.

To co-operate in creating and maintaining that sound public opinion and high idealism which make possible the increase of righteousness, justice, patriotism and good will.

L to R: back, Jeffery Dale Hudson, M. Snook, Sarah Hudson, Q.L. Snook; front, Earl Snook and Nicholas A. Hudson. 1990

Q.L. Snook, Jr., Q.L. Snook, III, Q.L. Snook, Sr., 1997

THE HONORABLE ORDER OF

𝕂entucky Colonels

— A TOAST —

I give you a man dedicated to the good things of life, to the gentle, the heartfelt things, to good living, and to the kindly rites with which it is surrounded. In all the clash of plangent world he holds firm to his ideal—a gracious existence in that country of content "where slower clocks strike happier hours." He stands in spirit on a tall-columned veranda, a hospitable glass in his hand, and he looks over the good and fertile earth, over ripening fields, over meadows of rippling blue grass. The rounded note of a horn floats through the fragrant stillness. Afar, the sleek and shining flanks of a thoroughbred catch the bright sun. The broad door, open wide with welcome . . . the slow, soft-spoken word . . . the familiar step of friendship . . . all this is his life and it is good. He brings fair judgment to sterner things. He is proud in the traditions of his country, in ways that are settled and true. In a trying world darkened by hate and misunderstanding, he is symbol of those virtues in which men find gallant faith and of the good men might distill from life. Here he stands, then. In the finest sense, an epicure . . . a patriot . . . a man.

Gentlemen, I give you, the Kentucky Colonel.

Kentucky Colonel Toast

Now that you have your book, you may want
to share a copy with a friend.
Special discounts will be quoted
for educational and sales use.

Send $18.95 plus $3.00 shipping and handling to:

Q.L. Snook, Sr.
Box 72, Savoy, IL 61874-0072
(217) 351-6998

or

Q.L. Snook, Sr.
756 Elkcam Blvd., Suite C
Deltona, FL 32725
(407) 574-4544